INFORMATION SEARCH GUIDE

C.J. Hunter-Brown and Anne Faulkner

MBA

Acknowledgement

We are particularly grateful to Una O'Sullivan for writing on 'Managing your information' (Section 2).

The Open University, Walton Hall, Milton Keynes MK7 6AA

First published 1998

Copyright © 1998 The Open University

All rights reserved. No part of this publication may be reproduced, stored in a retrieval system or transmitted, in any form or by any means, without written permission from the publisher or a licence from the Copyright Licensing Agency Limited. Details of such licences (for reprographic reproduction) may be obtained from the Copyright Licensing Agency Ltd, 90 Tottenham Court Road, London W1P 0LP

Edited, designed and typeset by The Open University

Printed in the United Kingdom by the Alden Group, Oxford

ISBN 0 7492 9280 6

Further information on Open University Business School courses may be obtained from the Customer Relations Centre, P.O. Box 222, The Open University, Walton Hall, Milton Keynes MK7 6YY

Contents

1 **Introduction** — 1
  1.1 Contents of this Guide — 1
  1.2 Study notes — 2
  1.3 'Top 15' sources — 4
  1.4 Case study: finding information on knowledge management — 5

2 **Managing your information, by Una O'Sullivan** — 6

3 **Library search technique** — 11

4 **Libraries and how to use them** — 13

5 **Sources of information: 'the basics'** — 17
  5.1 Books and how to trace them — 17
  5.2 Abstracts and indexes: finding journal articles — 19
  5.3 Journals – printed and online — 21
  5.4 Newspapers — 29
  5.5 Company information — 32
  5.6 Computer databases and the Internet — 37
    5.6.1 Searching databases — 39
    5.6.2 A selection of databases — 50
    5.6.3 The Internet — 59

6 **Sources of information: specialized areas** — 67
  6.1 Guides to information sources, subject bibliographies — 67
  6.2 The UK government and its publications — 68
  6.3 Standards — 71
  6.4 Patents — 72
  6.5 Statistics and market data — 73
  6.6 Trade literature and product data — 80
  6.7 Reports — 82
  6.8 Conference papers — 82
  6.9 Theses — 83

7 **Organizations** — 84
  7.1 Tracing organizations (directories) — 84
  7.2 Names and addresses — 87

8 **Case study: finding information on knowledge management** — 92

Index — 111

1 Introduction

1.1 CONTENTS OF THIS GUIDE

This Guide deals with the following topics:
- how to manage information;
- libraries and how to use them;
- types of printed information and how to find and use them;
- computer databases and the Internet and how to use them;
- organizations and how to trace them.

It is meant as a reference tool for use during your studies and perhaps at work. Of course, it is usually essential to review the literature in a field before embarking on a new project or dissertation. Also, at some stage in your studies you will probably need information beyond the scope of the course materials; you may want to read round your subject, investigate the background to a topic, or brief yourself quickly in some area that has become relevant to your work. You may need some quite specific piece of information to plug a gap in your knowledge, some technological fact or some set of market figures. You might want to trace a source of expertise in some other organization.

The Guide is fairly extensive in its coverage of information sources, but it is not, of course, exhaustive.

Section 2 gives you an overview of how to manage and apply the information that you assemble.

Section 3 contains some suggestions on search methods.

Section 4 deals briefly with libraries, their value and how to trace and use them.

The wide variety of sources of information are discussed in Sections 5–6. We have organized these sections largely according to the form of the sources. This is because the different kinds of publication tend to contain different types of information, which may be more or less up-to-date, more or less accessible, and so on.

We have called Section 5 'the basics'. It covers the first sources that a searcher would probably consult. However, the printed abstracts and indexes are being rapidly superseded by electronic sources: if you have easy online access to suitable databases, just skim through this section and look more closely at Section 5.6, which deals with electronic sources.

Section 6 can be viewed more as a reference resource. It covers more specialized areas, such as government publications and trade literature – consult them only if you need to.

Section 7 deals with how to trace information about a variety of organizations through directories and gives a selection of useful names and addresses.

Section 8 provides a 'worked example' or 'case study' of a sample search for information on knowledge management (see 1.4, below).

1.2 STUDY NOTES

'The literature' of a subject is traditionally viewed as the 'primary literature' and the 'secondary literature'. Individuals who produce the ideas and data may record them first in internal reports, journal articles and conference papers (the primary literature). Others may then summarize and organize the information directly, in handbooks, reviews, textbooks, encyclopaedias, and so on, or indirectly, in abstracts, indexes and bibliographies (the secondary literature). The records may be in printed or electronic form. All this is described, sorted out and signposted in sources such as libraries, printed subject guides and 'gateways' to the Internet.

Thus, for introductory and background information, for standard technical data, and so on, the less up-to-date, synthesizing sources will be the place to look: that is, encyclopaedias, textbooks, etc. To find a journal article on an industry, company or technology, you might turn to online databases or printed abstracts and indexes. But for information on research in progress or on the whole 'live' business area (new products, competitors' market shares), the more up-to-date, 'raw' sources will be appropriate.

So:

Theoretical, academic problems

If your problem is an academic one (for example, you may want to find a coherent summary of a management theory or to bring yourself up-to-date on recent developments in an area) then you could investigate the sources discussed in Section 5, 'the basics':

- 5.1 Books
- 5.2 Abstracts and indexes: finding journal articles
- 5.3 Journals – printed and online
- 5.6 Computer databases and the Internet

and even perhaps some of the sources in Section 6, 'specialized areas', such as:

- 6.8 Conference papers
- 6.9 Theses

Business queries

If your problem is more of a practical business one (you may, for example, want to find out how quickly a particular market is growing or to investigate the competition in an area of potential product diversification) then you could look at some of the sources mentioned in the following sections:

- 5 All 'the basics' could help, especially
- 5.4 Newspapers
- 5.5 Company information

    5.6 Computer databases and the Internet

and also 'specialized areas' such as:

    6.5 Statistics and market data

    6.6 Trade literature and product data

On the other hand, you might choose to approach an organization directly (Section 7 'Organizations').

These formal sources may not, of course, be the most important for you. Personal contacts and networks, or intuition based on your experience, may be more fruitful. But even if it is seen only as a second line of attack, a lot can be gained from a systematic use of the printed and electronic sources. Contacting individuals or firms you are not already familiar with can be quite time-consuming. A less complete or current picture gained from an electronic or printed source might prove adequate for your purposes.

General guidelines

Since any single piece of information is likely to be found in several places, there is no need to worry too much if you have access only to a limited range of sources (although in fact the reference collections of the county or city public libraries usually form impressively large 'databases'). The main thing to realize is that if you need some vital piece of information, you should be able to get at it somehow. **On the other hand, you should beware of getting bogged down or carried away in a search for a piece of information.** Research students might be able to spend months searching the literature, but when time is limited you should be aware of using up too much. There is a law of diminishing returns here. Getting the fullest possible answers to all your questions may take ten times longer than getting *adequate* answers to 80% of them. We encountered some of these pitfalls in a search for information on knowledge management which forms part of the case study in Section 8.

We would not like to be dogmatic about the time that you should set aside for information searching, but if, for example, you are writing a dissertation or doing the literature search for a project, you should probably be prepared to invest at least:

    a morning or an afternoon near the beginning of your project;

    a follow-up half-day later on;

    an hour or so from time to time for pursuing specific problems, making inter-library loan requests, etc.

Section 2 contains more advice on the issues involved in managing your information.

Remember too, when searching for information in libraries, to ask for help from librarians. They can save you a lot of time and trouble, simply by knowing their way around the shelves and the various catalogues and bibliographies (though naturally the first duty of librarians in a university or private institution will be to their own members).

Finally, note that the names and addresses of organizations sometimes change, and new editions of publications appear: inevitably, some of those mentioned in this Guide will become out of date.

1.3 'TOP 15' SOURCES

In this guide we have tried to provide advice on quite a wide range of information problems and we realize that consequently it can become rather hard for particular readers to extract the bits that will be personally useful to them.

Table 1 offers a short-cut – the 'Top 15' sources should produce solutions to most information problems. N.B. The guide has been written for Open University students. Some of the sources mentioned might not be available to people who are not OU students.

Table 1 'Top 15' sources	
Queries	**Sources (see index)**
Queries about books	
• how can I find *what has been published on my subject*?	WorldCat
• where can I *check incomplete references*?	WorldCat
• what's *available in bookshops now*?	Internet Book Shop
• what do people think of *this theory now*?	Social Sciences Citation Index
Queries about libraries	
• does my local university library take this journal?	Online library catalogues via NISS gateway
Queries about journal articles	
• where can I find references to *articles on this subject*?	Wilson Business Abstracts
	Social Sciences Citation Index
• I don't need a full bibliography, but can I get hold of the *full text of an article now*?	EBSCO MasterFILE
	BIDS JournalsOnline
• How have people *followed up* this piece of research?	Social Sciences Citation Index
• Where can I quickly find an article about the *international business position* of a product or service?	NISS Business and Industry Database
Queries about company information	
• where can I find the latest news on this company?	*Financial Times* (printed, CD-Rom, online)
	McCarthy (cards, online)
	NISS Business and Industry Database
• where can I find *financial data* on this company?	Directories in public libraries
	Biz/ed
	Business Information Sources on the Internet (Webber)
Exploring the Internet	
• how can I find *worthwhile sites*?	NISS NetFirst
	Biz/ed
	Business Information Sources on the Internet (Webber)
• Where can I find *online training* for improving my use of the Internet?	TONIC: the Online Netskills Interactive Course

1.4 CASE STUDY: FINDING INFORMATION ON KNOWLEDGE MANAGEMENT

In Section 8 we have included this 'case study' of searching for information to give an idea of what you might find in some of the information sources, how you might go about using them, and how much time searching them takes. Some people might like to get an idea of what this Guide is about by looking through the case study before the main body of the text.

Beginners at database searching might find it helpful to follow through one or two of the worked examples step by step at their own computers in order to gain an insight into the process of searching and practise with the mechanics of particular interfaces.

2 Managing your information

by Una O'Sullivan

Before launching yourself into a full-scale information search, it is useful to spend some time considering how you are going to manage your information throughout your project work. Gathering information from the variety of sources listed in this document is a time-consuming task; your aim, therefore, is to get the best return possible for this effort. This section aims to point out some of the skills and techniques that you can develop to manage your information effectively, and offers a short bibliography for more detailed information on this subject.

Knowing what you want

It may sound obvious, but having a clear idea of what you need to find out before beginning any kind of information search will make this process a lot easier to manage. Try to think of your project in terms of the information that you will need to gather. If you are going to use new tools such as databases, or software that you haven't tried before, recognize that you will also need information on how to use these tools. Try to estimate the time needed to use these various sources of information – this will help you to plan your project time more effectively.

Liz Orna (Orna and Stevens, 1995) recommends that researchers draw up a map which demonstrates both the 'territory' they are about to enter and the 'paths' needed to follow it through. By identifying the areas of knowledge that need to be investigated, the amount of knowledge that you already have and the most likely sources of information that you will need to use, this exercise will guide your information-gathering activities. It will also assist your 'filing' system, and should demonstrate how building up one area of knowledge will inform your work on another area.

While doing this, think also in terms of keywords. Many of the information gathering tools that students use, from bibliographic databases to the Internet, are searchable via keywords. Make a list of the most commonly used keywords in your field, and try, if possible, to expand this into a mini-thesaurus. This should be of significant benefit when it comes to doing keyword-based searches.

Recognising diverse sources of information

Information can be taken from a wide variety of sources: books, journals, conference proceedings, television programmes, the Internet, mailing lists, and so on. Use a diverse range of sources by all means, but know in advance the information that you will need to cite the resource correctly (see below). If you are using private or confidential information (e.g. company reports, correspondence), allow some time to obtain any necessary permission to incorporate that information into your coursework.

Don't forget to include other people in your list of information sources. Colleagues, fellow students and tutors may all be able to offer some information to support your studies, and it is helpful to develop your list of 'contacts' as soon as possible. Knowledge can be shared and distributed through teamwork, so if you do work in teams, make sure that you establish methods for saving and storing this knowledge. Even rough meeting minutes can prove to be a valuable source of information when it comes to producing coursework.

Finance

Be prepared to consider costs; some information services and products incur charges. In cases where you have a choice of paying or not (e.g. buying a book, or waiting a few weeks for your library to obtain it for you) try to weigh up the value of the service that you are paying for. If your need for the information is urgent, then it might be worth paying to have it sooner, if by doing so you can make faster progress with your work. If your need is less urgent, then consider your money in business terms – as a resource which might be better deployed elsewhere. If you are unsure as to whether a piece of information may be available at a reduced cost, or free, contact a librarian.

Developing your evaluation skills

According to Pacey (1995) the information literate should be able to access, evaluate, synthesize and communicate information. Tiefel (1995) defines information literacy as...

> 'the ability to access and evaluate information effectively for problem solving and decision making' (p. 326).

Critical thinking is a skill that is associated with evaluating information sources; it is intrinsic to information seeking behaviour. Atton (1994) explains that critical thinking is represented by the existence of:
- a readiness to question all assumptions;
- an ability to recognize when it is necessary to question;
- an ability to evaluate and analyse.

As you start collecting information for your project, be aware that you will need to develop your evaluation skills. You need to be able to tell very quickly whether a piece of information – e.g. an article in a journal, a web page – is worth spending more time on it. Try to develop a checklist of necessary or important features, which will help you to evaluate pieces of information. Some useful questions to ask yourself might include:
- Is the author known and respected in this field?
- Is reference made to other work in this field (e.g. does it demonstrate current awareness)?
- Is there a bias (political, personal) to this piece of information that affects the way that it is presented?
- Is the publisher of the information familiar/authoritative?
- Is the information properly referenced, i.e. is it possible for the reader to verify the points made?
- How current is the information? In the case of electronic information sources, is the information properly dated?

Working with your own checklist that is tailored to your own studies will help you to move more quickly and more efficiently through large amounts of information.

Recording your searches

The Golden Rule is to record your source information *as you find it*. Decide in advance what system you are going to use for citing your sources, and make sure that you note all the information that you need to keep to that system. For a book or journal article, note the publication date and details; note the pages, if appropriate, which are relevant to your studies. For a web page, note the full URL; find out the author's name, and the correct title of the resource, and note the date on which you last visited the page.

Whilst working online, it is especially important to record your searches properly, as this will save you telecommunications costs. Some practical information management techniques include:

- Keep directories for saving web pages and other electronic sources of information; one long list of HTML files will take a long time to search through if they are not properly ordered.
- Make sure that you save the copyright statement of the web page or web site, and any citation instructions as well.
- Make a note of the date on which you last visited the web page – this information is needed for references.
- If you need to contact the information provider, do this work offline. Make a note of the date and subject of your query – you may need to chase it.

You may wish to consider using a bibliographic software package, particularly if you are storing a large number of references on a computer. Packages include: *Pro-Cite*, *Reference Manager*, *EndNote Plus*, and *Papyrus* and *Bib/Search*.

Referencing/citations

Plagiarism is a major crime in the academic world! Therefore, ensure that you use references and citations to acknowledge all the information sources that you have used for your studies. As mentioned earlier, record your bibliographic information as you go; it is very time-consuming to go through notes trying to find information on all the sources that you have used.

When making a reference to a source, use the following examples as a guide to format:

Books

Author's surname, initial(s) (year of publication) *Title* (or Title), edition, publisher.

> Chen, M. (1995) *Asian Management Systems: Chinese, Japanese and Korean Styles of Business*, Routledge.

Journal articles

Author's surname, initial(s) 'Title of Article', *Title of Journal* (or Title of Journal), volume number, issue number, Date, pp ##–##.

Aaker, D. A. (1997) 'Should you take your brand to where the action is?', *Harvard Business Review*, vol. 75, no. 5, September-October, pp. 135-143.

Reports

Author's surname, initial(s) (date of report) *Title* (or Title), issuing organization, report number.

Clayton, J. and Gregory, W. (1997) *Total Systems Intervention or Total Systems Failure: Reflections on Application of TSI in a Prison*, Centre for Systems Studies, Hull University, HU-CSS-RM-15, Research memorandum no. 15.

Conference papers

Author's surname, initial(s) (year of publication) *Title* (or Title), Title of conference proceedings, date of conference, location of conference, pages on which the paper appears, publisher of proceedings, publisher's location.

Biel, A. L. (1992) *How Brand Image Drives Brand Equity*, Annual Advertising and Promotion Workshop, 4th, February 1992, New York, NY, pp. 163-178, Advertising Research Foundation, New York.

Electronic journal articles

Author's surname, initial(s) (year of publication) 'Title of article', *Title of journal* (or Title of Journal) [online], volume number, issue number. Available from: Name of Service, URL of website [date the site was accessed]

Bird, R. (1996) 'You need a translator or visual communication comes of age', *Deliberations* [online]. Available from: http://www.lgu.ac.uk/deliberations/ [Accessed 17 June 1997]

World Wide Web site documents

Author's surname, initial(s) (year of publication) *Title of document* (or Title of document) [online], publisher. Available from: Name of service, URL of website [date the site was accessed]

Reed Personnel Services (1997) *Over three-quarters of UK businesses now suffer from skills shortages* [online], Reed Personnel Services. Available from: http://www.reed.co.uk/editorial/trends29.htm [Accessed 8 January 1998]

Electronic mail messages

Author's surname, initial(s) (author's e-mail address), full date of message, *subject of message* (or subject of message). E-mail to recipient's name and e-mail address.

Knight, C. J. (c.j.knight@colc.ac.uk), 29 May 1997, *The year 2000 problem*. E-mail to j.q.parker-knoll@open.ac.uk

Knowing what you need to deliver

Keep in mind at all times what your final product will be (e.g. a report, a long essay, a project), and the implications that this has for your information management. If you need to include graphs or images, you may need some information on how to use the relevant software packages necessary to produce these. Consider the presentation of your work, and the best methods of presenting it (for example, it is sometimes easier to present statistical data in a graph rather than in a wordy paragraph). Deciding in advance the skills that you need for the presentation of your work means that you can plan the time necessary to acquire them.

Bibliography

Atton, C. (1994) 'Using critical thinking as a basis for library user education', *The Journal of Academic Librarianship*, vol. 20, nos. 5/6, pp. 310–313.

Cross, P. and Towle, K. (1996) A Guide to Citing Internet Sources [online], Bournemouth University. Available from: http://www.bournemouth.ac.uk/service-depts/lis/LIS_Pub/harvardsystint.html
[Accessed 19 November 1997].

Klare, G. (1979) 'Writing to inform: making it readable', *Information Design Journal,* vol. 1, no. 2, pp. 98–106.

Orna, L. with Stevens, G. (1995) *Managing Information for Research*, Open University Press.

Pacey, P. (1995) 'Teaching user education, learning information skills; or, towards the self explanatory library', *The New Review of Academic Librarianship*, vol. 1, pp. 95–103.

Tiefel, V. M. (1995) 'Library user education: examining its past, projecting its future', *Library Trends*, vol. 44, no. 2, pp. 318–338.

Tillman, H. (1997) *Evaluating Quality on the Net* [online], The Internet Access Company. Available from: http://www.tiac.net/users/hope/findqual.html [Accessed 19 November 1997].

3 LIBRARY SEARCH TECHNIQUE

This section deals with a comprehensive search for information in a library. If an academic type of literature survey is not appropriate to you, then skip it. (For the important field of online searching, see Section 5.6.)

These suggestions, too, are merely those that you might bear in mind, though for this sort of search it will certainly pay to be systematic. Your aim is to retrieve relevant information quickly and to avoid sorting through vast amounts of irrelevant material as much as possible. So first **identify, as clearly as you can, the questions to which you wish to find answers**, and then **define what it is you do not know**.

Table 2 is a checklist of the library search process.

Table 2	Checklist of library search process
Clarifying aims	What do you need to know to elucidate or develop your ideas?
Setting limits	How much *time* is it worth spending on the search? Set yourself a *time limit*. Is there a deadline?
	How *precise* need an answer be? Perhaps a rough answer will do?
	How *crucial* is a piece of information? (For example, is it *technically* crucial for the project's success? *Economically* crucial? Crucial from the *safety* or *industrial relations* point of view?)
	How *up-to-date* need the information be?
	How *comprehensive* need an answer be? (Stop when you have enough information or when you have reached your time limit.)
Introductory survey	Read up on background. Look in reference books (5.1).
	References: note down any useful-sounding references, introductory journal articles, books, and so on.
	Names: note down names of relevant organizations, authors.
	Abstracts and indexes: take a first look at one or two of the abstracts and indexes, in printed (5.2) or online (5.6) form.
	Keywords: if you think you will be searching in more detail later, note down keywords (terms used in indexes).
Choosing sources	Which sources will be used? In what order?
	Availability of sources: first work through appropriate sources that are easily available, for example in nearby public libraries, on your own bookshelf, or via your computer. Then, if specific problems arise, consider contacting or visiting a more specialized library or organization, preferably with a clear idea of the unique way in which they might be helpful.
	Subject approach: to what broad subject areas does the topic belong? Think of each aspect. For example, 'The

market for solar heating panels in south-east England' might involve broad fields, such as:

national energy policy;   market research;
local planning;   oil price trends;
technology;   meteorological data.
materials costs;

Type of information needed: what sort of source is likely to have the information in the form you want? If you are worried about the reliability of a piece of information, check it in more than one source.

Using sources

If you are using printed abstracts and indexes (5.2), begin with the most recent cumulation (an annual volume should give you a more complete idea of how a publication works than any single issue). Then go on to the most recent issues and work back.

Subject headings: work out the subject headings under which different aspects of your topic might be found: for example, 'small businesses' and 'decision making'. Then:

- discover the appropriate keywords;
- check synonyms or near synonyms ('solar cells' or 'photovoltaic cells', for example);
- check broader terms ('renewable energy sources');
- check narrower terms ('silicon solar cells');
- what about related fields (e.g. 'energy costs')?

If you are not making progress in a search, it will usually be because you have not hit upon the right keywords.

If you are using an online source, spend a little time exploring how to ask the system questions and how each entry is structured. Most databases have a 'subject heading' or 'descriptor' field. Again, think of synonyms, broader or narrower terms, related topics, and so on. Look at the descriptors used in the ways suggested in the paragraph above (and see Section 5.6.1).

Note relevant-sounding references and sources used (see 'Recording your searches' in Section 2).

Feedback (to check whether your search is on the right lines)

Obtain material: from shelves or on loan. Then decide:

- do these first articles suggest new approaches to the problem?
- do they contain further useful references? Key authors or papers might provide an entry point to a citation index (5.2);
- should you note any important organizations?
- are there any key journals emerging? Look at recent issues, or, if the journal is not available, at 'current contents', printed (5.2) or online (5.6);
- should you be prepared to modify your search ideas?
- need you go any further? Should you turn to another aspect of your project?

Then, consider the possibility of visiting a more specialized library. But, do not get carried away and spend too much time on a search.

4 LIBRARIES AND HOW TO USE THEM

Why use a library? Libraries contain a wide range of information sources, increasingly in electronic formats, although traditional libraries still have some advantages over electronic sources:

- they contain a huge volume of *'hard' information*;
- material is *systematically* and *consistently* organized.

It is worth spending some time investigating the reference collection of your local library. The reference collections of county libraries and the public libraries of the larger towns will often contain many of the sources listed in this Guide, including:

- abstracts and indexes (mentioned in Section 5.2). Using these, and following up with requests for loans and photocopies through the national inter-library loan service (see below), you have access to a huge amount of published work;
- collections of statistics, market data, trade directories, country profiles;
- CD-Roms (see Section 5.6 and elsewhere), particularly newspapers and business sources;
- Internet access, usually with a charge.

The more specialized abstracts and indexes (5.2) and the more sophisticated electronic formats (5.6) will be found in university and college libraries and in the specialized libraries of government departments and learned institutions. These bodies usually allow members of the public to use their collections for reference purposes, though policies do vary. There may well be a charge.

There are published guides to libraries (see below) and your tutor or OU regional centre will have details of the situation locally. You are automatically entitled to join public libraries in the counties where you live and work, but there will be a procedure to follow for becoming a member of other libraries. The OU Library is compiling a database of the services which UK university libraries offer to outside students, and at what cost, if any. When complete, the database will be accessible via the OU Library web pages:

> http://oulib1.open.ac.uk/lib/

With Internet access (see Section 5.6), you can save yourself wasted journeys by looking at the catalogues of university libraries online. You can find links to all UK university catalogues on the NISS gateway web pages:

> http://www.niss.ac.uk/

(choose 'Reference' and then 'Library OPACs (Online Public Access Catalogues) in HE').

Libraries in 70 countries are accessible from Berkeley Digital Library SunSITE's *Libweb: Library Servers via WWW*:

> http://sunsite.berkeley.edu/Libweb

The COPAC database offers 'one-stop' access to the combined catalogues of major UK and Irish university libraries:

http://copac.ac.uk/copac/

The catalogues of the British Library, including those covering science and technology and business, are available through the OPAC 97 service:

http://opac97.bl.uk/

In London, the Holborn branch of the **British Library's Science Reference and Information Service**, 25 Southampton Buildings, Chancery Lane, London WC2A 1AW (0171–412 7494) runs a **Business Information Service** (0171–323 7457). It has a comprehensive collection of abstracts and indexes, trade directories, trade and house journals, market surveys, patents, trade literature and company reports. It provides an online searching service and offers many databases on CD-Rom (see Section 5.6). Internet access to its catalogues is possible via the OPAC 97 service:

http://opac97.bl.uk/

The British Library's Document Supply Centre, Boston Spa, Wetherby, East Yorkshire LS23 7BQ (01937–843434), provides a lending service to other libraries or institutions (companies, public sector organizations, etc.). There is also a more expensive Copyright Cleared Service that supplies photocopies to individuals, who may either register and then pay £137.48 for 20 photocopied articles, or request photocopies of single articles of up to 50 pages for a charge of £15.86 (Customer Services: 01937–546060). The Centre's huge collection of journals, abstracts and indexes, conference proceedings, reports, etc. is open to the public for reference. Internet access to its catalogues is available via OPAC 97:

http://opac97.bl.uk/

The Export Market Information Centre (Department of Trade and Industry), Ashdown House, 123 Victoria Street, London SW1E 6RB (0171–215 5444/5) acts as a national reference library for the public use of overseas statistical series, market surveys, trade directories, development plans, and so on. The DTI's database, *BOTIS*, is accessible from all DTI Regional Offices.

The Business Information Centre, 64 Chichester Street, Belfast BT1 4JX (01232–233233) maintains collections of UK and overseas statistics, UK market surveys, trade journals and other sources of business information.

Perhaps the largest collection of business and company material is maintained in the **City Business Library**, 1 Brewers' Hall Garden, London EC2V 5BX (0171–638 8215), a public library intended to serve those who live, work or study in the City.

In Scotland, a business information service is provided by the **National Library of Scotland**, George IV Bridge, Edinburgh EH1 1EW (0131–226 4531), which has collections of trade and company directories, 400 industry files containing market research reports, cuttings, and so on, and 100 country files.

Other public libraries in London (Holborn, Westminster) and elsewhere (Birmingham, Cardiff, Manchester, Newcastle, Sheffield, and so on) are also important centres for business information.

Some of the professional organizations offer student memberships which include access to library services. For example, **The Institute of Management**, Management House, Cottingham Road, Corby,

Northamptonshire NN1 1TT (01536–204222) offers student membership at £35 (part-time students) or £25 (full-time). Services include free searching of IoM databases, loan facilities and photocopying.

Excellent coverage in the fields of health and social care policy, organization and management is provided by the **King's Fund Library**, 11-13 Cavendish Square, London W1M 0AN (0171-307 2568); open to the public by appointment.

Many of the organizations listed in Section 7 have libraries specializing in various aspects of technology or business. Obviously it is wise to contact a government departmental library or a private organization beforehand to find out whether a visit is possible and might be worthwhile.

Listed below are guides to libraries, with information on availability to outsiders, opening hours and, most usefully, subject coverage. Using their indexes, you can locate libraries specializing in your subject:

Aslib Directory of Information Sources in the United Kingdom (1996) 9th edn, Aslib.

Guide to Libraries and Information Units in Government Departments and other Organisations (1996), 32nd edn, British Library.

Guide to Libraries in Key UK Companies (1993) British Library (all the libraries listed are willing to answer queries from outsiders).

Guide to Libraries in London (1995) British Library (detailed information on 1,000 libraries).

World Directory of Business Information Libraries (1993) Euromonitor.

Further details on specialized libraries may be found in appropriate guides to information sources (Section 6.1).

Using libraries

(Regular users of libraries may want to skip these notes.)

To find books on a given topic

Nowadays, library catalogues are online and there will be menus or web interfaces on the screen to guide your search. When you find useful-sounding books, make a note of the *classification number* or *shelf-mark* and go straight to the shelves – just browsing can be valuable. Or, if you want a complete list of what the library has on your topic, you can look at the entries for those books that are classified at the same number (choose the appropriate option from the screen menu). If the book you want is out on loan, the library will reserve it for you.

Remember that books that might be of interest to you may not be shelved together. However exhaustive a classification might be, a single book may be looked at from many points of view, but can only occupy one place on the shelf. Table 3 is an example from the Dewey Decimal Classification of how books on computers and computing might be dispersed on the shelves.

Again, the screen display will guide you in the search for books by a certain author or issued by a particular organization.

So:

> *master the catalogue*;
>
> *browse*;
>
> if in difficulties, *consult the librarians*.

Table 3	An extract from the Dewey decimal classification system
Classification	**Dewey No.**
Computers: Bibliographies	016.004
Computers: Data security	005.8
Computers: in Decision-making	658.4030285
Computers: Human factors	004.019
Computers: Law and legislation	342.64
Computers: Management applications	658.05
Computers: in Manufacture of products	670.427
Computers: Networks	384.3
Computers: Office practices	651.8
Computers: Purchasing	001.64040687
Computers: Social aspects	306.46
Computers: Software exporting	382.450053

To obtain material not in your library

Most public libraries will forward requests for books, journals, journal articles, reports, and so on, not in their possession, to other libraries co-operating in a regional inter-library loan scheme, or to the British Library Document Supply Centre at Boston Spa. You might receive books or journals on loan, or photocopies of individual articles (which you keep).

The process can sometimes take a long time, particularly in the case of books, so if you can foresee the need to look at a particular item, *put a request in as early as you can*. However, the service from the Document Supply Centre is usually very speedy. If you wish to establish your own link with the DSC, see the note above in this section. Otherwise, public libraries will usually forward requests for you – my own public library system accepts requests at any branch library and charges from 65p to £1.

If there is a library in your own organization, this might be one of the most useful services they could offer you. Many of the professional institutions (Section 6) offer student members lending and photocopying services. Photocopied journal articles usually cost about £3 each.

Some online databases (Section 5.6) offer facilities for ordering photocopies or faxes of articles. However, they tend to be expensive (about £8 an article) and they usually ask you to give your credit card details online.

Finally, authors are sometimes willing to supply reprints of recent articles. Printed indexes and computer databases usually include information on authors' institutional affiliations.

When applying for a loan, you should give full bibliographic details (see 'Recording your searches' in Section 2).

5 Sources of Information: 'The Basics'

5.1 BOOKS AND HOW TO TRACE THEM

If you want to brief yourself on some business or management topic and do not mind if the account is not absolutely up-to-date, then you will probably look first in an encyclopaedia or textbook. Articles in encyclopaedias or chapters of textbooks may also be useful for the references they contain to classic papers and books.

As well as some of the general reference works, such as *The New Encyclopaedia Britannica* (32 volumes), most libraries will have a few more specialized ones. Often one of these will contain as much as you may want to know about a subject, in a convenient form:

Dodgson, M. and Rothwell, R. (eds) *The Handbook of Industrial Innovation* (1996) new edn, Edward Elgar;

The Financial Times Handbook of Management (1995) Pitman;

Gower Handbook of Management (1995) 3rd edn, Gower;

International Encyclopedia of Business & Management (1996) 6 vols, Routledge.

Otherwise, look for the textbooks and readers recommended in the course material and browse the shelves – and see the notes on 'Tracing books' below.

Reference books covering business data are dealt with in the appropriate sections below (e.g. in Section 5.5, *Company information*, Section 6.5, *Statistics and market data,* and so on). The larger public libraries have impressive collections.

Dictionaries

For enquiries regarding terminology, there are many specialized dictionaries, such as:

Bennett, P.D. (1995) *Dictionary of Marketing Terms*, 2nd edn, NTC Business Books;

A Dictionary of Finance (1993) Oxford Reference, Oxford University Press;

Friedman, J.P. (1994) *Dictionary of Business Terms*, 2nd edn, Barron's;

Gunton, R. (1993) *A Dictionary of Information Technology and Computer Science,* 2nd edn, NCC Blackwell (also issued as *The Penguin Dictionary of Information Technology)*;

Johannsen, H. and Page, G.T. (1990) *International Dictionary of Management,* Kogan Page;

Paxson, D. and Wood, D. (1997) *Blackwell Encyclopedic Dictionary of Finance,* Blackwell

Statt, D.A. (1991) *The Concise Dictionary of Management,* Routledge

Acronyms and abbreviations have their own dictionaries, from the vast, such as:

> *Acronyms, Initialisms and Abbreviations Dictionary* (1997) 22nd edn, 3 volumes, Gale Research;

to the more manageable, such as:

> King, G. (1994) *Dictionary of Abbreviations and Acronyms,* Mandarin, in association with the Sunday Times.

Dictionaries are also beginning to appear on the Internet (see Section 5.6.3).

For instance, 220 dictionaries can be searched at:

> http://www.onelook.com/

If in the end you cannot easily find what you want in a book, you can turn elsewhere, to abstracts and indexes (Section 5.2), to journals (Section 5.3), to reports (Section 6.7) and so on.

Tracing books

If you are in a library, look in the catalogue (Section 4) and browse among the shelves. Most libraries have separate reference collections, so encyclopaedias, handbooks and dictionaries may be shelved away from textbooks.

Look for bibliographies in the books you have already found and look for relevant subject bibliographies.

If you want an idea of the books available on a given subject, or if you need to trace full details of half-remembered books, libraries keep various comprehensive bibliographies such as:

> *British Books in Print* (Whitaker's);
>
> the *British National Bibliography*;
>
> the annual G.K. Hall *Bibliographic Guides*, such as:
>
> > *Bibliographic Guide to Business and Economics.*

Ask the librarian about these.

Among online sources (Section 5.6), *WorldCat*, from OCLC FirstSearch (free to Open University students), is a huge database with over 36,000,000 references to books and other media.

The Internet Book Shop contains records of nearly a million books in print in the UK. You search the database via a well-designed web interface (at the opening screen, click on 'search for a book') and useful books can be ordered online:

> http://www.bookshop.co.uk/

You can also trace books by using online library catalogues – see Sections 4 and 5.6.

Of course, many journals list and review books, the *Financial Times* produces a regular supplement reviewing new books, and the larger booksellers such as Blackwell's, Dillon's or Heffer's, issue useful subject lists.

5.2 ABSTRACTS AND INDEXES: FINDING JOURNAL ARTICLES

If you cannot find what you are looking for in books, you can try to find a journal article on the subject.

You may already be keeping an eye on a few favourite journals, but abstracts and indexes give you indirect access to thousands more articles and publications. In their printed or, increasingly, electronic versions (Section 5.6), they will probably provide your main way into the published sources of information. With their help you should be able to pursue a topic through the literature or find a recent article on a subject you are investigating without too much trouble. Even if you do regularly see one or two good journals, it is worth looking at a couple of the main indexes (printed or electronic) from time to time. A researcher scanning only a few core journals may well miss interesting material appearing elsewhere.

Note that the methods and layout of these indexes vary greatly, making use of broader or narrower headings, different keywords, synonyms, spellings, and so on. Where they give abstracts (short summaries of the full article) these may themselves contain useful information and give you an idea of whether a reference is worth following up, either by going to the shelves or by applying for an inter-library loan. Online access (Section 5.6) can be a great time-saver, of course, and in many libraries is replacing printed indexes: *so if you have access to a suitable database, try the electronic route first.*

You will probably have to visit a specialized library, that of a university or professional body for example, in order to find most of the printed indexes listed here. We have indicated which of the indexes can be searched online via a computer terminal (*); which can be searched online without charge for OU students (^{OU}); and which are also available on CD-Rom (^{CD}); turn to Section 5.6 for more on these.

Business and management

$^{*,\ CD}$ Anbar abstracts, Anbar Electronic Intelligence (various specialized series which include only articles 'considered important': *Accounting and Finance Abstracts, Information Management and Technology Abstracts, Marketing and Distribution Abstracts, Operations and Production Management Abstracts, Personnel and Training Abstracts* and *Top Management Abstracts*; consolidated annually, with indexes, in the useful *Compleat Anbar*);^{CD} *British Humanities Index,* Bowker-Saur (indexes over 300 British journals, some newspapers and the general weeklies; includes social sciences, economics and some management; quickly searched and useful for current affairs and general economic and business topics; CD-Rom *BHI Plus*);

$^{OU,\ CD}$ *Business Periodicals Index,* H.W. Wilson (340 journals, worldwide; indexes subjects, industries, companies; quickly searched; American bias, but useful; also covers some theoretical management; online version via OCLC FirstSearch is *Wilson Business Abstracts*);

Management and Marketing Abstracts, Pira International (aims to inform management and marketing executives of worldwide developments in the theoretical and practical areas of their activities; includes all areas of management, not just marketing);

* *Market Research Abstracts,* two a year, Market Research Society (long abstracts and detailed subject index);

*,CD *Predicasts F and S Index Europe ,* Information Access (new products, new capacities, product end uses and market data; Section 1: Industries and products (classified in detail); Section 2: Countries; Section 3: Companies; the entries may themselves contain useful figures. Similar Predicasts indexes cover the United States of America and the rest of the world);

*,CD *PROMPT: Predicasts Overview of Markets and Technology,* Information Access (very comprehensive coverage of developments in all industries, worldwide; abstracts in broad industry arrangement with detailed product indexes; cumulated quarterly and annually);

*, CD *Public Affairs Information Service Bulletin,* PAIS (business topics are extensively covered, with emphasis on economic factors, management policy-making, business–societal interactions and similar broad issues; indexes journals, books and government documents; easy to use);

* *Research Index,* Business Surveys (100 British trade and professional magazines and newspapers; listings of articles by industry and a few broad subjects, then A–Z by company; up-to-date and useful for its coverage of trade journals and for the latest news of industries and companies; available at

http://www.researchindex.co.uk/beta/search.htm);

OU, CD *Social Sciences Citation Index* (see below: 'Citation indexes');

OU, CD *Social Sciences Index* (indexes 350 journals).

A convenient source for actual articles from the financial press is the *McCarthy Information* cuttings service (also available online and as CD-Rom). The cuttings, reproduced on cards and arranged by company, and/or the CD-Rom, are found in many libraries.

Technology

* CD *Abstracts in New Technologies and Engineering,* Bowker-Saur (covers British and American journals, including trade journals; useful for finding quick up-dates on technical developments; CD-Rom *ANTE plus);*

* CD *Catchword and Trade Name Index,* Bowker-Saur (spin-off of *Abstracts in New Technologies and Engineering*; indexes catchwords, jargon, product names and names of businesses, so can be useful for the sort of precise topics it is often difficult to track down elsewhere: you can look up things like 'Salter's Duck', 'Wind Energy Group', and so on; CD-Rom *ANTE plus);*

With regard to more specific subject areas, there are many specialized abstracting services which you will find in appropriate special libraries (see Section 4).

Citation indexes

There is a special category of index, the citation index, that should be mentioned.

Instead of using subject headings, the *Science Citation Index* and the *Social Sciences Citation Index* (published by the Institute of Scientific Information) base their indexes on the references that appear at the end of journal articles.

These indexes tell you who has referred to a particular book or paper. You look up a key paper or book in the Citation Index section. Here you will see a (highly abbreviated) list of articles that have included the book or paper in their bibliographies, and where, therefore, you can assume that some aspect of your subject is discussed. The Source Index contains full details of the citing papers. This can be a very fruitful approach.

If you would like to try a citation search, you are strongly recommended to do it via BIDS on a computer. For that reason, we will discuss the search methodology in more detail in Section 5.6.1, 'Searching databases'.

Current contents

If you want to keep track of what is appearing in the latest issues of a journal or review publication which you do not have to hand, then the 'current contents' type of publication will help. By reproducing contents pages, they fill the time gap between publication of a journal and the indexing of its articles in the abstracts and indexes. They usually have keyword subject indexes. If you come across a likely-sounding article, you can then obtain it as a photocopy via the inter-library loan service. Examples include:

Contents Pages in Management, fortnightly, Manchester Business School;

Current Contents: Social and Behavioral Sciences, weekly, Institute for Scientific Information.

Online (5.6), you can go to the OCLC FirstSearch system and select *ContentsFirst*, which gives the contents pages of 12,500 journals in all fields, or you can go to *Social Sciences Citation Index* on BIDS (choose 'Journal title' on the Advanced Search screen).

At the time of writing (November 1997), BIDS is planning a service, AutoJournals, where the contents pages (and abstracts if wanted) of journal issues which you select are e-mailed to you as soon as they are entered on the BIDS system. Look at the BIDS home page for details:

http://www.bids.ac.uk

5.3 JOURNALS – PRINTED AND ONLINE

Although searching printed indexes and online databases is the best way of tracking down what has been written on some particular topic of interest, it is also essential to keep abreast of what is going on in your field by regularly scanning one or two journals.

We have divided the list of journals that follows into two groups: 'academic', for theoretical articles on aspects of management, and 'news', for reports on current affairs, business matters, technological innovations, conferences, and so on. Of course the division is somewhat arbitrary.

Many of the magazines in the second group are not only useful for keeping up to date, but also carry articles that are certainly of academic interest. Trade journals and specialist practical magazines can be very useful sources of articles on 'the state of the art' in their fields, and are often the best providers of up-to-date information on new products and processes, markets and statistical trends.

You will already know of journals in your own field, but, because there is such a huge variety of specialized academic or trade journals that might be useful in different contexts, we have added a note on tracing journals at the end of the section. (Further details of subscriptions, addresses, and so on, of the journals listed can also be found in the sources given there.)

Increasingly, the full texts of journals are available electronically. For more information on this important resource refer to 'journals online', at the end of this section.

Management – general

Academy of Management Journal, six a year, Sheridan Press (research articles of interest to members of the Academy of Management)

Academy of Management Review, four a year, Sheridan Press ('rigorous, conceptual papers that advance the science and practice of management')

Administrative Science Quarterly, quarterly, Johnson Graduate School of Management ('dedicated to advancing the understanding of administration through empirical investigation and theoretical analysis')

British Journal of Management, quarterly, Blackwell Publishers ('research and scholarship on management oriented themes and topics')

California Management Review, quarterly, Haas School of Business, California University ('a bridge of communication between those who study management and those who practise it')

Columbia Journal of World Business, quarterly, Columbia University

European Management Journal, bimonthly, Elsevier Science ('practical approach to the latest thinking and research on major management topics')

Harvard Business Review, six a year, Harvard University (highly respected journal for professional managers).

Journal of Business Research, 9 a year, Elsevier Science (theory applied)

Journal of General Management, quarterly, Braybrooke Press with Henley Management College

Journal of Management, bimonthly, JAI Press ('results of research that either provide solutions to problems or enhance opportunities for public and private organizations')

Journal of Management Studies, bimonthly, Blackwell Publishers (all aspects of management research, from empirical studies and theoretical developments to practical applications)

Management Decision, eight a year, MCB University Press (general management and strategy issues for managers, consultants, teachers and students)

Management Learning, quarterly, Sage ('international journal for managerial and organizational learning and development')

Management Science, monthly, Institute for Operations Research and the Management Sciences ('innovative research and novel applications for today's decision makers')

Omega, bimonthly, Pergamon ('developments in management, including research results and applications')

Sloan Management Review, quarterly, Sloan School of Management (best current management theory and practice, with a particular emphasis on corporate strategy, organizational change, and management of technology)

Finance & accountancy, economics

Accountancy, monthly, Institute of Chartered Accountants

Accounting, Organizations and Society, eight a year, Pergamon ('behavioural, organizational and social aspects of accounting')

Critical Perspectives on Accounting, bimonthly, Academic Press ('for social and organizational accountability')

Journal of Accountancy, monthly, American Institute of Certified Public Accountants

Journal of Business Finance and Accounting, 10 a year, Blackwell Publishers (aims to 'advance the academic understanding and professional practice of effective financial management, control and accountability')

Journal of Economic Literature, quarterly, American Economic Association (guide to research and publications)

Journal of Finance, five a year, American Finance Association (respected academic journal)

Journal of Industrial Economics, four a year, Blackwell Publishers (economic analysis relating to the problems of the market economy through theoretical and applied work in the field of industrial organisation)

Management Accounting, monthly, Chartered Institute of Management Accountants (for professionals and students)

Management Accounting Research, quarterly, Academic Press

Human resources

British Journal of Industrial Relations, four a year, Blackwell Publishers

Evaluation Review, six a year, Sage Periodicals Press ('a journal of applied social research')

Human Resource Management, quarterly, Wiley (for effective problem-solving and decision-making in the human resource field)

Human Resource Management Journal, quarterly, Institute of Personnel and Development

Industrial Relations Journal, four a year, Blackwell Publishers

Journal of Applied Psychology, bimonthly, American Psychological Association (including business-related applications such as job performance and analysis)

Journal of Human Resources, four a year, University of Wisconsin Press

Innovation, strategic management, technology management, R & D

Creativity and Innovation Management, four a year, Blackwell Publishers (aims to extend understanding of creativity through testing practical experiences against emerging theories)

Futures, ten a year, Butterworth–Heinemann ('journal of forecasting and planning', including methodologies and national policies)

International Journal of Technology Management, 16 a year, Inderscience Enterprises (aims to facilitate communication between government, managers in industry and academics)

Long Range Planning, six a year, Pergamon (innovation policy, planning and forecasting techniques in industry and government; 'current awareness' section of abstracts of recent articles)

R and D Management, quarterly, Basil Blackwell (management of innovation; market research; effects of government policies; expert systems)

Research Policy, quarterly, North–Holland

Strategic Management Journal, monthly, Wiley (for practising managers and academics)

Technology Analysis and Strategic Management, quarterly, Carfax (links 'the analysis of science and technology with the strategic needs of policy-makers and management')

Marketing

Journal of Marketing, quarterly, American Marketing Association

Journal of Marketing Research, quarterly, American Marketing Association

Journal of Marketing Management, eight a year, Dryden Press (aims to 'fill the middle ground between the academic journals and the trade press')

Marketing Science, quarterly, Institute for Operations Research and the Management Sciences

Organizational studies

Organization Science, bimonthly, Institute for Operations Research and the Management Sciences

Organization Studies, bimonthly, Walter de Gruyter ('an international multidisciplinary journal devoted to the study of organizations, organizing, and the organized in and between societies')

Organizational Behavior and Human Decision Processes, monthly, Academic Press ('a Journal of Fundamental Research and Theory in Applied Psychology')

Organizational Dynamics, quarterly, American Management Association (application of the behavioural sciences in organizations)

Research in Organizational Behavior, annual, JAI Press ('series of analytical essays and critical reviews')

Public sector

Public Administration Review, bimonthly, American Society for Public Administration

Public Finance Quarterly, quarterly, Sage Publications (allocation, distribution and stabilisation functions in the public sector)

Public Money & Management, quarterly, Blackwells Publishers (reviews policy, finance and management)

News (for newspapers, see Section 5.4)

Business Week, weekly, McGraw-Hill

^{CD} *Economist*, weekly, Economist Newspaper Ltd (excellent source of economic and business information, with useful sections on management)

^{CD} ENDS *Report*, monthly, Environmental Data Services (excellent source of political, legislative and technological news on all aspects of the environment)

Engineer, weekly, Morgan–Grampian (industrial, technological and political news for engineering management; articles on new technologies, materials, products and management of innovation)

Engineering, monthly, Gillard Welch Associates ('for innovators in technology, manufacturing and management')

Forbes, fortnightly, Forbes (sections include: 'Management, Strategies, Trends', 'Money & Investments' and 'Technology')

Fortune, fortnightly, Time, Inc. (American-oriented; some useful surveys of business and technological developments)

Management Today, monthly, Haymarket Publications (general magazine for managers; sometimes includes articles on innovation, marketing and so on)

There are far too many of the often very useful specialized trade or professional journals to list here, but see the sources in 'Tracing journals' below.

Tracing journals

After looking in the periodicals collection of the library you normally use, you could ask if there is a local 'union catalogue': that is, a listing of all the journals taken by libraries in the area. Alternatively, you could visit one of the libraries mentioned in Section 4, or look at their catalogues online.

You might get an idea of worthwhile journals in a field with which you are unfamiliar by looking up the subject in the abstracts and indexes (Section 5.2), doing a brief computer search (Section 5.6) or by looking in a specialized guide to information sources (Section 6.1). Many publishers will send sample copies.

The general guides to periodicals:

Ulrich's International Periodicals Directory, R.R. Bowker;

Willing's Press Guide, Hollis Directories;

are found in nearly all libraries. They include addresses, subscription rates, and so on.

A useful list, particularly for people who can visit the Science Reference and Information Service library in Holborn, is:

> Barrett, D. (1996) *Business Journals at SRIS*, British Library.

There is a list of British trade journals arranged in order of Standard Industrial Classification numbers (that is, the official government classification of industries) in:

> Tudor, J. (1992) *Macmillan Directory of UK Business Information Sources*, 3rd edn, Macmillan.

Worldwide coverage is provided by:

> *World Directory of Trade and Business Journals* (1996) Euromonitor.

Journals online

Many journals are now available online: you can bring up the full text of articles on your screen. Some of these journals are published only electronically and they vary widely in quality. Others are electronic versions of well-known printed publications. Sometimes access is free, sometimes a charge is involved. Often special software must be installed to read both text and figures. You can find out more by following up the sources given below in the section 'Tracing electronic journals'.

EBSCO MasterFILE

The OU Library subscribes to the EBSCO MasterFILE, a collection of over 1,000 journals, and this is available to OU students. Contents can be searched by keyword, and complete articles read on screen or printed out. The collection is not at all academically comprehensive – anyone doing academic research would have to turn to the large bibliographic databases such as BIDS. However, the collection does provide you with the opportunity to find one or two complete articles from respected magazines – *Forbes, Fortune, Economist*, and so on – containing up-to-date information and ideas on topics of interest to you. Access is easy and does not require special software, but diagrams and photographs cannot be seen. The following are some of the journals you can access via the EBSCO MasterFILE:

Accounting Review	Economic Systems Research
Administration and Society	Economist
Administrative Science Quarterly	Forbes
	Fortune
American Economic Review	Futurist
Bankers Magazine	Group and Organization Management
Business America	
Business and Society	Growth and Change
Business Economics	Industrial and Labor Relations Review
Business Quarterly	
Business Review	Information Systems Management
Columbia Journal of World Business	Innovation

International Studies of Management and Organization

Journal of Accountancy

Journal of Advertising

Journal of Business and Economic Statistics

Journal of Business and Technical Communication

Journal of Consumer Affairs

Journal of Economic Issues

Journal of Education for Business

Journal of Environmental Planning and Management

Journal of International Business Studies

Journal of Labor Research

Journal of Management Accounting Research

Journal of Management Education

Journal of Management Information Systems

Journal of Management Inquiry

Journal of Marketing

Journal of Marketing Research

Journal of Public Policy and Marketing

Journal of Small Business Management

Journal of Socio-Economics

Journal of the Economics of Business

Leadership

Manage

Management Accounting

Management Quarterly

Management Review

Managers Magazine

Marketing Management

Marketing News

Marketing Research

Marketing Tools

McKinsey Quarterly

Money

Nation's Business

Organizational Dynamics

Personnel Journal

Personnel Psychology

Public Personnel Management

Public Relations Quarterly

Total Quality Management

Training and Development

Women in Business

You need to register (by returning the OU form *Use of Copyright Databases*, see Section 5.6). You can then access the file by following the route provided on the OU Library's web pages

http://oulib1.open.ac.uk/lib/

Once you have reached the 'NISS EBSCO' page:

1 Click on 'Search MasterFILE'.

2 Enter the Username and Password issued to you on registration and click on 'OK'.

3 Choose a subject collection, e.g. 'Business and Economics', 'Public Affairs and Law', by clicking in the adjacent circle (it is not possible to search the whole database at once).

4 Scroll down to enter your search (you can scroll further down the page for advice) and click on 'Search'. (N.B. *Searches in the 'Article text' can take a long time – a one or two word search in the 'Article title' or 'Abstract' box or a single (significant) word search in the full 'Article Text' will speed things up.*)

5   You will then see a list of article titles, arranged under each journal's name; click on a promising title and you will be able to see the complete article; articles can be printed out using your browser or saved to your own computer (save as a text file, e.g. **innovation.txt**).

You can also use your passwords to search the *Business and Industry* database. This indexes 880 business and trade journals covering a broad range of industries world-wide; it contains over 500,000 records and is updated daily. Over 60% of the records provide the full text of the articles. (Refer to 'computer databases and the Internet' (Section 5.6) for further details):

http://www.niss.ac.uk/b+i/

BIDS JournalsOnline Full Text Service

The full texts of all journals published by Academic Press and of those published by Arnold, Blackwell Publishers and Blackwell Science to which the OU subscribes, are available to OU students via the BIDS JournalsOnline Full Text Service. You can search the database as a whole to find articles on a particular subject or by a particular author, or you can read (or print off) the complete contents of individual issues.

Here are some of the titles that might interest business and management students. New titles are constantly being added to the list.

Annals of Public & Cooperative Economics	Journal of Environmental Economics & Management
British Accounting Review	Journal of Environmental Management
British Journal of Industrial Relations	Journal of Financial Intermediation
British Journal of Management	Journal of Industrial Economics
Creativity & Innovation Management	Journal of Management Studies
Critical Perspectives on Accounting	Journal of Vocational Behavior
Games & Economic Behaviour	Management Accounting Research
Gender, Work and Organization	New Technology, Work & Employment
Industrial Relations Journal	
International Journal of Advertising	Organizational Behavior & Human Decision Processes
International Journal of Selection & Assessment	Public Administration
	Public Money & Management
Journal of Business Finance & Accounting	World Economy

As with the EBSCO MasterFILE, you need to register (by returning the OU form *Use of Copyright Databases,* see Section 5.6). You will also need to download and install the free Adobe Acrobat software and to configure your browser accordingly (you only need to do this once – the system will thereafter automatically bring the software into action when it is needed). Full instructions are available via the OU Library's home pages at

> http://oulib1.open.ac.uk/lib/

Using the Adobe Acrobat software, you see the article as it appears in printed form, complete with illustrations, formulae, etc. Printed out, an article resembles a conventional reprint.

Once you have the Acrobat reader correctly installed:

1. click on your web browser's icon and in the Location box type

    > http://www.bids.ac.uk

2. click on 'BIDS *JournalsOnline* Full Text Electronic Journals Service'
3. click on 'registered users', enter your BIDS Username and Password and click on 'login';
4. you can then:

    either search the whole collection of journals by filling in the search form on the screen

    or you can click on 'Browse' (top left) to go directly to the contents of particular journal that interests you;

    Note the 'Help' *button;*
5. if a title looks interesting, click on 'details';
6. if you then wish to see the full text of an article, click on 'document availability'; if you are offered free delivery, just click on 'deliver document'.

Note: if you are accessing the service from a commercial ISP, you may then find yourself at the Academic Press Ideal site where you will be asked for a further username and password – you will have been notified of these with your other passwords.

Tracing electronic journals

If you would like to go beyond the journals in the collections of the EBSCO MasterFILE and BIDS JournalsOnline service, you could start by looking for an 'electronic journals' category in appropriate Internet gateways (see Section 5.6.3). Sometimes, too, you will find electronic journals listed with other web sites under the various subject headings.

Many hundreds of titles are listed in the *ARL Directory of Electronic Publications* which can be accessed via:

> http://www.gold.ac.uk/history/hyperjournal/hyperj.htm/

The *Ejournal SiteGuide: A MetaSource* and the searchable archive of *NewJour: Electronic Journals and Newsletters* provide direct links to electronic journal sites and to individual titles:

> http://www.library.ubc.ca/ejour/
> http://gort.ucsd.edu/newjour

5.4 NEWSPAPERS

The *Financial Times* offers the most comprehensive coverage of British and international business and also regularly issues, as supplements, comprehensive surveys of countries and of various industries, particularly in areas such as:

information technology;

telecommunications;

office automation.

Part 2 of the newspaper, 'Companies and markets', is obviously a prime source of company information. Furthermore, company case studies are regularly described on its 'Management' page. The daily 'Technology' page provides a handy way of keeping an eye on new products and processes and offers good briefings on technological developments (company addresses and telephone numbers are included). Other regular features cover 'Business and the environment', 'Marketing and media', 'Accountancy' and 'Business education'. New management books are reviewed in a separate supplement.

Coverage of business and technological issues in other papers is not as thorough, though *The Guardian* covers policy issues well. The *Financial Times* and the *Daily Telegraph* run information services (on subscription).

Many libraries have complete sets of *The Times, Sunday Times* and *The Guardian* on microfilm. Most will keep runs of a year or so of these, of other Sunday papers and of the *Financial Times*. The microform sets will be supported by printed indexes.

Indexes to newspapers

Apart from the indexes to individual newspapers mentioned above, more comprehensive coverage is found in:

CD * *British Newspaper Index*, quarterly (CD-Rom index to *The Times, Sunday Times, Financial Times, Independent* and the *Times Supplements*; from 1990 onwards);

CD *Clover Newspaper Index*, weekly, Clover Publications (covers the *Daily Telegraph, Economist, European, Financial Times, Guardian, Independent, Observer, Sunday Times* and *Times*; a widely found, up-to-date and detailed index; publishes a *Company Data Supplement* which turns into the annual *Companies in the News*);

* *Research Index,* fortnightly with cumulations, Business Surveys (a business-oriented index to the *Daily Express, Daily Mail, Daily Telegraph, Financial Times, Guardian, Independent, Observer, Scotsman, Sunday Express, Sunday Telegraph, Sunday Times* and *Times,* plus trade and professional journals; listings of articles by industry and a few broad subjects, then A–Z by company; available at http://www.researchindex.co.uk/beta/search.htm).

In addition, the *British Humanities Index* covers major feature articles.

The more substantial supplements and special reports on industries or countries published in the British press are indexed in:

Index to Business Reports, biannual, Quarry Press (indexes special supplements and surveys from about 30 newspapers and magazines; can be useful for following developments in an industry back through time).

Newspapers on CD-Rom and online

An increasing number of libraries now subscribe to CD-Rom versions of the broadsheet newspapers (see Section 5.6 for a general discussion of electronic and online sources). The CDs usually come out quarterly, until a whole year is contained on one disk. Searching a CD-Rom is of course much easier than searching through printed indexes and microfilm. When you find useful articles, they can be printed out in full or saved on to floppy disk. Many public libraries now stock some of these CD-Roms and we also indicate in the list below which ones are available in the Business Information Service (BIS) of the Science Reference and Information Service (SRIS):

The Financial Times (Financial Times Information/Chadwyck-Healey) (1988–on; available at BIS/SRIS);

The Guardian (Chadwyck-Healey) (1990–on);

The Independent (Financial Times Information/Chadwyck-Healey) (1989–on; available at BIS/SRIS);

Le Monde (Primary Source Media) (1992–on);

Il Sole 24 Ore (BIG CD-Rom/Chadwyck-Healey) (1988–on);

The Daily Telegraph and *The Sunday Telegraph* (Financial Times Information/Chadwyck-Healey) (1991–on);

The Times and The Sunday Times (News Multimedia) (1990–on);

The Wall Street Journal (European and Asian Editions) (UMI)

FT Profile and other hosts offer the full texts online of UK and overseas newspapers back to the early 1980s, but at a highish price.

Online versions of the current issue of some newspapers, together with free searchable archives, are available on the Internet. At the time of writing (November 1997), *The Times* and *Sunday Times* for 1996 on and the *Telegraph* from November 1994 on are available. The *Financial Times'* site offers highlights of the current day's issue and a searchable archive of a month or two. The situation is very fluid: a good place to start in order to see what's available now is the NISS Information Gateway (for the UK academic community):

http://www.niss.ac.uk/

and then:

1 click on 'News';
2 click on 'Newspapers and news sources by region: – United Kingdom';
3 click on 'Electronic Telegraph', 'Times and Sunday Times', 'Financial Times', etc. …;
4 at the newspaper's home page, look for 'search', 'archive' or 'library' and follow the instructions.

For a worldwide listing of online newspapers, you can go to the useful *Editor & Publisher* site, again via the NISS Information Gateway ('News' and then 'Collections of online newspapers').

A useful source for investigating newspaper coverage of a company is:

*, CD McCarthy Information Ltd. offers original articles from the financial press, on cards, arranged by company. This convenient press-cuttings service is found in many public libraries, often in CD-Rom format (*McCarthy,* Financial Times Information/Chadwyck-Healey; also available at BIS/SRIS).

5.5 COMPANY INFORMATION

You may need to find information on companies or to use companies as sources of information. Many companies may be willing to discuss management practice or their markets and products. Students have tended to find the larger companies more geared to providing this sort of information than the smaller ones. Obviously, problems of commercial or technological confidentiality might arise.

Directories

There are very many directories indexing companies by product or place, or giving more or less detailed administrative and financial information on them. Some of them provide rankings lists which can be useful for 'placing' companies in their industrial sector or region. Below are a few of the most commonly found directories. Many more are listed in the 'Guides to information sources' (Section 6.1) and in the guides to directories (Section 7). An increasing number of the larger directories are now found also in electronic formats (Section 5.6).

The Company Guide, quarterly, Hemmington Scott (up-to-date summaries of activities, largest shareholders, 5-year financials for all UK stockmarket quoted companies);

Corporate Financial Performance, 2 volumes, annual, Dun & Bradstreet (eleven key figures abstracted from the companies in *Key British Enterprises*);

CD *D and B Europa,* annual, 4 volumes, Dun & Bradstreet (names and addresses and basic financial data; covers most European countries; Europe-wide company rankings by turnover, employees; lists top companies in each business sector ranked by turnover);

*, CD *Key British Enterprises,* annual, Dun & Bradstreet, 6 volumes (the top 50,000 British companies, SIC and geographical indexes, British business rankings, Trade names, Export markets, Directors' names);

*, CD *Kelly's,* annual, Reed Information Services ('yellow pages' listings of 82,000 manufacturing and service companies);

Key Business Ratios, annual, Dun & Bradstreet (20 key ratios covering three years for 370 industry groups)

*, CD *KOMPASS UK,* annual, Reed Information Services (also issues volumes covering 45 other countries; particularly detailed product indexes; geographical listing, financial data, parents and subsidiaries, industrial trade names, quality assessed companies);

Macmillan Stock Exchange Yearbook, Macmillan (4,409 companies, including all listed companies and securities; directors, subsidiaries, company history, financial data, 5-year financial summary, substantial shareholders, recent capital history);

Macmillan's Unquoted Companies, annual, Macmillan ('profiles of Britain's top 20,000 unquoted companies'; 'Industry League Tables' rank companies by Return on Capital Employed);

The Times 1000, annual, Times Books (rankings and analysis; also includes Europe's top 100, North America's top 100, Japan's top 100, and the Australia, New Zealand and Southeast Asia top 100);

Whiteside, R. M. (ed.) (1995) *Major Companies of Europe 1995–96,* Graham & Whiteside,

Company interconnections are dealt with in:

*, CD *Who Owns Whom,* 5 volumes, annual, Dun & Bradstreet (lists parent companies with subsidiaries, and indexes subsidiaries; covers UK, Continental Europe, North America and Australasia and the Far East).

Names of directors can be found in most of the above directories and also in the widely found:

Directory of Directors, annual, Reed Information Services;

Who's Who in the City (1996) Macmillan.

Many of the commercially produced industry and market surveys mentioned in Section 6.5 also serve as excellent directories for their sectors.

For abstracts and indexes as sources of information on companies, see Section 5.2.

For newspapers as sources of information, see Section 5.4. Obviously the *Financial Times* will be a prime source of company information, and in public libraries you will find at least some of the indexes described in Section 5.4, such as the *Clover Newspaper Index* and its *Company Data Supplement*, and the *Research Index*. The *Research Index* is now available on the web at:

http://www.researchindex.co.uk/beta/search.htm

More information on directories and other sources of company information can be found in the guides listed in Section 6.1.

Financial data and news

For financial data, large public libraries will carry one of the frequently up-dated, card-based (or, nowadays, CD-Rom) services, such as Extel's or McCarthy's (actually a press-cuttings service, see Section 5.4). Most of the directories listed above give basic financial data, as do some of the market surveys (Section 6.5).

The Companies Registration Office keeps the files of statutorily required information on all companies (which of course covers more than just financial data). Addresses of Companies House and its satellite search rooms are as follows:

Cardiff: Companies House, Crown Way, Cardiff CF4 3UZ (01222–388588)

Birmingham: Central Library, Chamberlain Square, Birmingham B3 3HQ (0121–233 9047)

Edinburgh: 37 Castle Terrace, Edinburgh EH1 2EB (0131–535 5800)

Glasgow: 7 West George Street, Glasgow G2 1BQ (0141–221 5513)

Leeds: 25 Queen Street, Leeds LS1 2TW (0113–233 8338)

London: 55–71 City Road, London EC1Y 1BB (0171–253 9393)

Sets of the Companies House microfiche sets – or at least their information request forms – are sometimes found in public libraries, or you can telephone the Central Enquiry Unit on 01222–380801. Search-room services, post, fax and courier search services, and the Companies

House Direct On-line service are offered. Further details and a full list of prices can be found at the Companies House web site:

http://www.companies-house.gov.uk/

Information taken from the register is also available via added-value commercial computer-based services, such as *FAME* and *ICC* (see Section 5.6). The *FAME* CD-Rom (Bureau van Dijk and Jordans) (available at the Business Information Service at the SRIS) contains financial data from Companies House on 100,000 companies, plus 30 business ratios. Analytical and graphics capabilities enable you to compare a given company's financial variables with its industry norms or with its individual competitors; statistical analysis is also offered; data can be downloaded to spreadsheets. CD-Roms in the same series cover Europe (*AMADEUS*) and Japan (*JADE*).

Detailed financial information covering sales, balance sheet, share data, business ratios, etc., is contained in the *Disclosure Worldscope* and *Disclosure United States* CD-Roms kept in the Business Information Section.

Annual reports prepared by public companies for their shareholders may contain up-to-date information on strategy, future plans, and so on. Two useful CD-Roms (again kept in the Business Information Service at SRIS) contain company annual reports and accounts, and stockbroker reports:

InvesText (Information Access Company);

UK Company Factfinder (Knight-Ridder Information).

The Internet

The Internet is becoming an increasingly fruitful source of company information. Many of the gateways mentioned in Section 5.6.3 will lead you to company sites. For example, *Business Information Sources on the Internet* has sections covering 'trade directories', 'company directories' and 'company profiles and financial information':

http://www.dis.strath.ac.uk/business/index.html

and *Biz/ed* hosts *Extel Data* which provides financial data (20 key variables), and three year company profiles (click on 'Data' at the Biz/ed home page) of 500 well known companies:

http://bizednet.bris.ac.uk:8080/home.htm

Directory-style information on companies, and company news and financial data (worldwide) can be found at the *Financial Times* site:

http://www.ft.com/hippocampus/contents.htm

(you will need to register online, with no charge, via the following URL prior to accessing the URL above)

http://www.ft.com/cgi-bin/ft/register.pl/

The web sites of some of the UK's largest companies can be accessed through the list of FTSE 100 companies:

http://www.ftse.com/ftse_100.html

The Fortune 500 home page can be accessed from the Engineering Information Village (Ei Village):

http://www.ei-village.org.uk/village/

Click on the 'Business and Financial District' icon, then select Fortune 500.

Sites offering share price information (subject to a 20 minute delay on the free services), including in some cases five year price profiles and other information and news relevant to equity prices, include Electronic Share Exchange, Yahoo (with links overseas) and UK Equities Direct:

> http://www.esi.co.uk/
>
> http://finance.yahoo.co.uk/
>
> http://www.hemscott.co.uk/hemscott/

The BIZ is useful for those seeking UK-relevant business information, products and services. This site is essentially an index of associations, companies and organizations, providing their addresses and other contact details, including web sites where relevant.

> http://www.thebiz.co.uk/info.htm

The addresses of many US companies can be searched for via *Companies Online*. It is also possible to browse by industry subject categories. Additional company information, such as annual sales, employee size and company trade name(s), can be searched for by those who register (free of charge).

> http://www.companiesonline.com/

Europages: The European Business Directory provides a searchable database which lists 150,000 European suppliers. The database can be searched either by free text (for products/services) or by 'theme' (type of industry) or 'company name'.

> http://www.europages.com/home-en.html

CAROL (Company Reports Online) provides free access to European Company Annual Reports. This site can be searched alphabetically, and by category.

> http://www.carol.co.uk/

The *Millennium UK Business Directory* lists the addresses and telephone numbers of over 60,000 UK companies. It is searchable by company name (A–Z) and by sector.

> http://www.milfac.co.uk/milfac/

Gateways concentrating on special fields can also be helpful: for example, the *EEVL* gateway (engineering and technology) allows you to limit your search to 'Commercial servers' and then specify a particular sector:

> http://www.eevl.ac.uk/

BRINT: A Business Researchers Interests, is a gateway which lists links to sites under various headings, including 'Business and technology,' from which you can find links to company and business information sources.

> http://www.brint.com/interest.html

BizInfo: A guide to conducting business research on the Internet, lists web sites. Sites are categorized under headings including company profiles and company directories.

> http://www.hbs.edu/applegate/bizinfo3/

The Harvard Business School's Baker Library maintains a gateway to business and management resources on the Internet. It has company and industry information sections.

http://library.hbs.edu/

Other specialized services, such as *DIAL* and *Engineering UK*, allow you to do subject (product) searches for companies:

http://dialindustry.co.uk/
http://www.engineering-uk.co.uk/

Trade associations and research associations

Trade associations can be very useful sources of information and data about their industry, although since they are formed and financed by individual companies to represent their interests, they may be wary about releasing information given in confidence. They may issue a yearbook, collect and publish statistics, and so on.

Research associations aim to benefit their member companies by providing the technological expertise, research results, advice and information they could not generate on their own. They are financed and controlled by their members, although many have technical and contractual links with an appropriate government department. There are about 50 industrial research associations, including:

Motor Industry Research Association;

PERA (Production Engineering Research Association);

RAPRA (Rubber and Plastics Research Association).

Both these types of organization usually have well organized libraries and information centres. Even if you do not have access to them through individual or company membership, they are often open to members of the public for consultation of material not available elsewhere.

Trace them through an appropriate trade directory or through the general directories, such as: *Associations and Professional Bodies of the United Kingdom* and *Industrial Research in the United Kingdom* (see Section 7). There is the specialized:

World Directory of Trade and Business Associations (1995) Euromonitor.

For European associations, there are:

Directory of European Industrial and Trade Associations (1991) 5th edn, CBD Research;

European Directory of Trade and Professional Associations (1990) Euromonitor.

Chambers of Commerce

Chambers of Commerce can be useful sources on information on small companies in their areas. The national association is:

Association of British Chambers of Commerce, 9 Tufton Street, London SW1P 3QB (0171–222 1555).

You can find Internet links to UK Chambers of Commerce at the DIAL site at:

http://www.dialindustry.co.uk/

5.6 COMPUTER DATABASES AND THE INTERNET

Below are sections on 'Searching databases', 'A selection of databases' and 'The Internet'. The Internet section contains basic advice on searching the Internet, using search engines and gateways and evaluating sources, and ends with a short list of some sites which should make useful starting-points.

Many abstracts and indexes, such as those marked with an asterisk in Section 5.2, and an increasing range of newspapers and journals, are available for online searching. Online searching is fast and it offers the capacity to specify a subject in great detail. You can download the results to your own computer for editing and later printing. Many databases are also stored on CD-Roms searchable via a network, or on a single machine fitted with a CD-Rom drive. A lack of funds available to individual libraries for maintaining paper collections on the one hand, combined with the increasing sophistication and accessibility of electronic sources on the other, means that computer databases are becoming increasingly important to the researcher.

The Open University, on behalf of its students and staff, subscribes to various databases, the most important and easily accessible being the bibliographic databases offered by BIDS and OCLC FirstSearch (see Section 5.6.2, below) and the collection of journals in full text offered by the EBSCO MasterFILE and the BIDS JournalsOnline Full Text Service (see Section 5.3). In addition, the Internet offers a vast number of potential sources of information.

The Open University has negotiated a special rate for Internet access with the Internet service provider U-Net. Students are sent forms for forwarding to U-Net. Those who wish to use BIDS, OCLC FirstSearch, EBSCO MasterFILE and some other databases mentioned in this Guide should also fill in and return the form *Use of Copyright Databases*. Information about access, including passwords, will then be made available to them via the FirstClass conferencing system. (If registration to FirstClass is not part of a course routine, students can apply for the pack to Learning Materials Sales, P.O. Box 188, The Open University, Walton Hall, Milton Keynes MK7 6DH; tel. 01908 655955; e-mail: LMS-admn@open.ac.uk).

Of the databases below, those marked [OU] are available for searching by Open University students. Some (those marked [CD]) are issued as CD-Roms and might therefore be found in appropriate libraries. Searching CDs is often free, though there will probably be a charge for pages printed out. In the list below, we have indicated where a CD is available for free searching in the Business Information Service (BIS) of the Science Reference and Information Service (SRIS). Many other public and university libraries carry a useful range of CD-Roms, although some university libraries restrict access by outsiders.

Searching remote databases other than those available to you through the OU usually involves a charge, paid either to the database host or to an intermediary such as the SRIS. Various 'hosts', such as the European Space Agency (ESA-IRS), FT PROFILE and Knight-Ridder Information (DIALOG and Datastar), offer a range of 'files' for searching.

Arrangements regarding payment, password, and so on, have to be made with these hosts (unless, of course, you are searching through an intermediary, either in a library or in the form of a network service such as CompuServe or Demon). Costs depend upon:

1. the amount of time you spend connected to the computer;
2. the number of references, abstracts, articles or sets of figures you have printed out.

Often there is no subscription: you pay only for actual use. A search will typically cost between £15 and £60.

Here are some addresses of organizations that offer business and management services and a range of databases.

Knight-Ridder, recently acquired by MAID plc, are now operating under the name: The Dialog Corporation Plc. The Dialog Corporation's head office address is: The Communications Building, 48 Leicester Square, London WC2H 7DB (tel: 0171–930 6900, URL: http://www.dialog.com/).

FT Discovery is a subscription-based online business information service. It covers company and market sector information. FT Discovery, 13–17 Epworth Street, London, EC2A 4DL (tel: 0171–825 8000). FT Profile, which offers a wide range of newspaper, market research and financial databases, and FT Discovery have the same parent organization, Financial Times Information Ltd, which can also be contacted at the above address.

Datastream is an investment-orientated online information and data service which is charged for (expensive). Datastream, Skandia House, 23, College Hill, London EC4R 2RA (tel: 0171–398 7751).

Reuters is an online financial data and news (including real time) service (expensive). Reuters, 85 Fleet Street, London EC4P 4AJ (tel: 0171–250 1122).

Many of the UK organizations who use these online information retrieval services will do searches for the public. They may pass the charges directly on to the outside user or make a fixed charge. The SRIS's Business Information Service offers cost-plus computer searches, charging £80 an hour plus online cost.

Some public libraries offer a subsidized service. The Institute of Management's Information Centre will search its own databases (see below) free for members. Student membership of the Institute costs £25 (full-time students) or £35 (part-time). If you are a member of a professional institution, it would be worth finding out what is on offer to you in the way of database searching.

CD-Roms are usually paid for on a subscription basis (normally several hundred pounds a year), but thereafter searches are 'free'. For example, SRIS's Business Information Service makes no charge for searching, but does charge for pages printed out (40–60p per page) or downloaded (£10 per floppy disk – though this is not always permitted). An advantage of doing a search at the SRIS is that many of the references retrieved will actually be found on the shelves. It might well be worthwhile to find out what CD-Roms are available to you locally.

The information available from databases is not only bibliographic but also includes series of statistics, well-known business directories, the complete texts of newspapers, magazines and business reports, information on current research projects, etc.

A number of databases offer financial and trading information about industries and companies. Some (e.g. *FAME*) offer financial data taken from Companies' House or annual reports, plus analytical software. A company's performance can be compared with that of rival companies and with industry averages, the results being displayed graphically. Although business files tend to be rather expensive, they can produce information quickly that is not easily available elsewhere on such topics as company finances and markets.

5.6.1 Searching databases

Just as with the printed indexes, each electronic database has its own characteristics. The same warnings apply regarding differences in indexing policy and so on, with the added complication that search interfaces vary from host to host and from CD-Rom to CD-Rom. However, although the detail varies from database to database, the underlying concepts remain the same. Also, unlike in the case of printed indexes, a computer search need not be restricted to the file's own index terms: you can ask the machine to retrieve references with any given word or phrase in the title, abstract, or full text.

If you are not already a regular user of a system and you want to run a computer search, you may need to set aside an hour or so for it. If someone else is doing the search for you, you will need to discuss exactly what you want and how it is best to be expressed at the terminal. You should be there when the search is run. You will be able to respond in the light of the papers your search is producing and amend the profile until the results look right. If you are searching for yourself, you will need some time to get used to the system you are using and to experiment with different keywords.

Logging on to BIDS, OCLC FirstSearch, and Business and Industry Database via NISS

BIDS

1. Open your web browser and in the 'Location' box, type:
   http://www.bids.ac.uk
2. Scroll down and click on the words 'BIDS Web Search Services', then on the database you require (e.g. 'ISI Citation Indexes', 'Ei Compendex / Page One', etc. – see Section 5.2).
3. Enter the Username and Password issued to you.

OCLC FirstSearch

1. Open your web browser and in the 'Location' box, type:
   http://www.ref.uk.oclc.org:3000/
2. Click on 'Use FirstSearch'.
3. Enter the Username ('Authorization') and Password issued to you.
4. Choose a broad subject category, highlight the database you require and click on 'Select Database'.

Business and Industry Database (Via NISS)

1. Open your web browser and in the 'Location' box, type:
   http://www.niss.ac.uk/
2. Click on 'ATHENS Subscription Services', then click on 'NISS Business & Industry Service'.

3 Click on search and then 'advanced search'. Submit your search by clicking the 'search' button. If your search is successful you will be presented with a list of article titles.

4 You will be asked for a Username and Password once per session, after you have clicked on the first article title that you are interested in.

Searching by using keywords

When you are doing a search, the computer, in effect, scans through the whole file, setting aside all papers that have been tagged with given 'descriptors' (index terms), or that contain certain words or phrases. Words or phrases can be combined logically. For example, if you were looking for something on the marketing of personal computers, you might first ask the system to assemble a set of articles with a microcomputer-type word or phrase in the title, abstract or index field (e.g. Computers, Personal Computers, PCs) and then to assemble a set with marketing-type words (Marketing, Markets, Advertising). Finally, you ask it to combine the two sets and print out the resulting set. This will consist of articles where both concepts are covered, that is, records that have at least one of the computer words and one of the marketing words.

So the secret of effective searching is *to choose the right keywords and combine them in a logical way.* Here is how you might prepare a search strategy for yourself or for an intermediary to follow. (You might not be quite as systematic as this, but even if you are doing a search yourself with no constraints of time or money, you should certainly try to keep the logic of what you are doing clearly in mind):

1 What subject do you wish to investigate? Write it down in a single sentence: 'Evaluation of marketing strategies in the public sector'.

2 Break the topic down into broad concepts: you are going to be assembling keywords into broad subject groups, so clarify what the central concepts of the topic area are.

3 Don't overdo this: you will probably find that it breaks down into only two or three broad concepts (e.g., 1. Evaluation, 2: Marketing, 3: Public sector).

4 Put the concepts into order of importance: one or two concepts will be vital, others less so (for example, 'references retrieved must concern evaluation and they must concern marketing strategies, but they need not necessarily deal with the public sector').

5 For each concept group, list synonyms of the keywords: be precise; don't stray too far from your original concept

6 Think of the words different authors might have used in their titles to express various aspects of the topic (don't forget American spellings).

7 Is there a very specific word or phrase you might like to be found (the name of an organization? A product name?): if so, write it down.

8 Investigate the index terms – or 'descriptors' or 'controlled terms' – used by the database. These comprise a controlled collection of words and phrases which the indexers must use to describe the content of each article in a consistent way. By expressing your search request in the terms used by the database:

- You are less dependent on divining the exact words used by individual authors.

- You are less likely to pick up irrelevant references retrieved because of some passing use of a word (in an abstract for example).
- Of the databases available to OU students through BIDS, *Ei Compendex* and *Ei Page One* work through a thesaurus, the citation indexes do not: the OCLC FirstSearch databases nearly all work with a (fairly basic) set of descriptors; searches of Business and Industry Database can be limited by region (country) and industry terms.

Either

if you are working in a library where the printed thesaurus of the database you are using is available:

- look up likely keywords or phrases
- follow up cross-references to narrower terms (NT), broader terms (BT) and related terms (RT)
- make a note of all promising-sounding terms: each must be specified separately

Or

- find the descriptors used by the database by looking at entries *online*
- if you are using a CD-Rom, follow the instructions on the screen for looking at the thesaurus online: note the promising-sounding terms
- or, experiment with a few likely keywords and display the titles found until you find a useful article: then display the full entry and look carefully at that part of the entry where the index terms appear (they might be called 'Descriptors', or 'Controlled Terms' or 'Subject Headings', etc.)
- make a note of the promising-sounding terms and follow these up: continue the process until you are satisfied you have explored the system thoroughly.

Finally:

9 Check the logic:

you might try writing out your request in full:

'Find articles which have:

1. any one of: *either* Evaluation *or* Effectiveness *or* Assessment, *AND*,
2. any one of: *either* Marketing *or* Promotions *or* Market strategy.'

Does it make sense?

Are all the words in the right concept groups?

10 Another way of looking at this process of combining terms logically is to think in terms of 'Boolean operators' (that is, 'AND', 'OR', 'NOT'). Here is the diagram for AND:

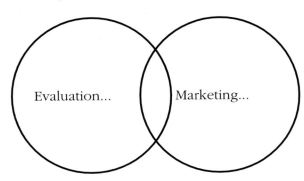

Think of the 'evaluation' set of keywords in the first circle, the 'marketing' set in the second. What you want is the intersection, references that contain one of the 'evaluation' words AND one of the 'marketing' words.

N.B. Some searching systems allow you just to type out 'and', 'or', etc. However, on BIDS the operators are represented by the following symbols (and see the 'Hints' table below):

Boolean operators in BIDS

AND	+	
OR	,	
NOT	–	(be careful with this)

To ensure search terms are grouped correctly, each concept group should be enclosed in brackets – think of the brackets as equivalent to the Boolean circles above.

Sample search

- (evaluation or effectiveness or assessment) and (marketing or promotions or market strategy)

  or, in 'BIDSpeak':

- (evaluation,effectiveness,assessment)+(marketing,promotions, market strategy)

The example below illustrates the use of Boolean logic to combine search terms.

Documents are required on managing conflict within an organization. Terms which represent the same concept should be grouped together in columns:

managing	AND	conflict	AND	organization
		OR		OR
		dispute		company
		OR		OR
		discord		association

Terms that represent the same concept should be linked using the OR operator. Terms representing different concepts (occurring in separate columns) should be ANDED together.

11 *Warning*: as well as AND/OR, you can use NOT. However, this can be dangerous: for example, asking for **UK NOT USA** will exclude 'A comparison of public sector marketing policies in the UK and USA': it is probably best to restrict the use of NOT to excluding from your current set those references that you have already seen in previous sets.

12 Most databases will allow you to take account of plurals, different verb forms, etc. By using 'truncation' or 'wild-cards', you can ask for all words with a given stem. *Business and Industry* Database and databases on BIDS use an asterisk for this: **market*** will retrieve 'market', 'markets', 'marketing'. OCLC FirstSearch uses a plus sign, but here only plurals are allowed for: **market+** will retrieve 'market' and 'markets' but not 'marketing'.

13 Databases vary in how you are required to enter phrases. Some (on BIDS for example) will allow you to type in the phrase as it stands. Other databases require an 'operator' to indicate that it is a phrase. When using OCLC FirstSearch, 'w' is this operator, hence: the phrase 'market research' would be entered as: **market w research**. Some databases, such as EBSCO Masterfile, use inverted commas, hence: **'market research'**. If you are in any doubt about which operator (if any) to use then consult the particular database's online 'help' section.

14 After you have entered a search, the system responds by telling you how many 'hits' it has produced. For example, after you have entered a search on BIDS and clicked on 'Run the search', a message appears: 'The system found 67 (or whatever) hits':

- if this number is enormous, you will need to refine your search by adding further requirements, e.g. by adding **+(public sector, hospital*, nonprofit*)** (you might imagine you were looking through a printed index at titles listed under one of your top priority keywords: what further words or phrases would catch your eye as you looked through the list?).
- if very little is found, you would broaden the search by being less demanding in your requirements (e.g. by expanding your list of alternative keywords, or by dropping an entire list of qualifying terms).

Assembling your bibliography

When you have a manageable number of hits (up to about 150, say), scroll through the list 'checking' (by clicking in the adjacent boxes) references that look interesting – in effect the system will be putting these on one side for you to display later or to e-mail to yourself (see below 'Transferring your bibliography to your own computer').

N.B. With reference to BIDS, records are displayed in batches of 30 – before clicking on 'Next Page', *you must click on 'Mark Checked Articles'* or your bibliography will be lost.

The system on OCLC FirstSearch is similar, but instead of 'checking' and 'marking' references, you 'tag' and then 'save' them – see Table 5, 'Searching on OCLC FirstSearch: some hints' later in this section.

Transferring your bibliography to your own computer

When you have assembled your bibliography of promising-looking references, you can (on BIDS):

- *either* click on 'E-Mail Marked List' and fill in the electronic form – the bibliography will be sent to your computer via your e-mail address; this method produces the neatest result;
- *or* click on 'Display Marked Articles' and use your browser to print them out or save them to your own computer: i.e. those using Netscape would click on 'File' at the top left of the screen, select 'Save As' and give the file a name with a 'txt' suffix, e.g. **market.txt**

Or (on OCLC FirstSearch):
- to receive up to 20 tagged records by e-mail, select 'Show these tags' and follow the instructions.

Finding journal articles via citation searching

If you know of a core paper in your field, do not forget that a way of minimizing problems of vocabulary is to use this paper as a basis for a 'Citation search' (see 'Citation indexes' in Section 5.2). *Social Sciences Citation Index* is available to you via BIDS and a citation search can often be very worthwhile.

Why do a citation search?

- The citation approach can turn up relevant articles from unexpected disciplines.
- You are not dependent on the author's or indexer's choice of vocabulary.
- Instead of starting with an article and working *back* in time by following up the references given at the end, citation searching provides you with a way of searching *forward* in time. It allows you to follow up discussion and argument, to see *what happened next*.

How to do a citation search

The citation indexes offer an indexing system based on the references that appear at the end of all the journal articles on the database. This approach tells you who has referred to a particular book or paper. For example, if you were interested in design methodology, you might choose Jones, J.C. (1980) *Design Methods: Seeds of Human Futures,* 2nd edn, Wiley, as your 'target' book. A citation search will give you a list of all the articles on the database that have included Jones's book in their bibliographies, and where, therefore, you can assume that some aspect of design methodology is discussed.

For instructions on how to get through to BIDS, see above. At the opening screen, click on 'Search ISI Database' and at the screen 'BIDS ISI Easy Search':

1. Click on 'Citation Search' and a screen 'BIDS ISI Citation Search' will appear.
2. Select either Science Citation Index or Social Sciences Citation Index by clicking in the box 'Using citations from the ... database'.
3. Enter the name of your target author in the prescribed format (**Jones_JC**) and the year of publication (owing to the inconsistent way that people cite their references, it is usually best not to fill in more than your author's name and the year of publication of the book or paper, unless it is a very common name); then click on 'Run the search'.
4. The system responds with a list of the books and papers published by Jones in 1980 which have been cited in the bibliographies of the articles in the database.
5. Often your 'target' book or paper will have been cited in several different ways – click in the boxes next to these various versions to 'check' the reference you are after (as in the list below) and then click on 'Retrieve articles which cite the checked references':

Copyright 1997, Institute for Scientific Information Inc.

- ❏ JONES_JC, 1980, Vol.26, CUTIS (4 refs)
- ❏ JONES_JC, 1980, DEC P INT S PROBL PR (1 refs)
- ☑ JONES_JC, 1980, DESIGN MEHODS SEEDS (1 refs)
- ☑ JONES_JC, 1980, DESIGN METHODS (3 refs)
- ☑ JONES_JC, 1980, DESIGN METHODS SEEDS (8 refs)
- ❏ JONES_JC, 1980, Vol.74, FIRE J (3 refs)
- ❏ JONES_JC, 1980, Vol.73, SO MED J (5 refs)

6 The computer responds with a list of 12 articles which cited Jones's book and therefore might be of interest to you:

(1) TI: SYSTEMS AND DESIGN AS THE BASIS OF ENGINEERING KNOWLEDGE
AU: KORN_J
JN: IEE PROCEEDINGS-A, 1989, Vol.136, No.2, pp.87-94

(2) TI: THE STRUCTURE OF DESIGN PROCESSES
AU: DASGUPTA_S
JN: ADVANCES IN COMPUTERS, 1989, Vol.28, pp.1-67

(3) TI: OPPORTUNISTIC SOFTWARE ARCHITECTURE FOR SUPPORT OF DESIGN COORDINATION
AU: MACCALLUM_KJ, CARTER_IM
JN: KNOWLEDGE-BASED SYSTEMS, 1992, Vol.5, No.1, pp.55-65

(4) TI: MODELING KNOWLEDGE-BASED SYSTEM FOR OPTIMUM MACHINE-DESIGN
AU: KOWALSKI_J
JN: MECHANISM AND MACHINE THEORY, 1992, Vol.27, No.4, pp.491-505

(5) TI: CONCEPTUAL FOUNDATIONS OF DESIGN PROBLEM-SOLVING
AU: SMITH_GF, BROWNE_GJ
JN: IEEE TRANSACTIONS ON SYSTEMS MAN AND CYBERNETICS, 1993, Vol.23, No.5, pp.1209-1219

etc. etc.

You can then 'check' interesting-sounding articles as in a keyword search (and again, do not forget to 'Mark checked articles').

Summary, and tables of 'Hints' for using BIDS, OCLC FirstSearch, and Business and Industry Database

CD-Roms and many of the remote database hosts are usually web or windows-based and therefore to a large extent intuitive to use. Older interfaces employ a 'menu' system, a structured system of prompts and available options. The user frames requests as suggested by the menus on the screen (but a careful consideration of the words you use and the logic with which they are combined is still the key to successful searching). It is usually possible to get good results without much difficulty and if you run into trouble, there is usually a clue to the solution somewhere on the screen.

The BIDS system incorporates more sophisticated possibilities for logical searching than does OCLC FirstSearch, although OCLC is gradually introducing greater refinements. BIDS issues brief explanatory leaflets which are also available electronically on the BIDS Internet pages:

> http://www.bids.ac.uk

More formal training material can be found on the OU Library's web pages

> http://oulib1.open.ac.uk/lib/

Remember that systems provide online Help: you can click on the 'Help' button or, in the case of BIDS and others, you can click on the hypertext links on the search form (e.g. on the highlighted word 'Author') and get context-sensitive help. Note that *Business and Industry*'s 'Help' button is in the form of a white question mark on a red background.

A few hints to searching on BIDS, OCLC FirstSearch, and *Business and Industry* Database follow below and we give examples of a couple of straightforward searches of databases in the Case Study (see Section 8). You might like to get a feel for searching by following through the steps of those searches yourself.

Finally, bear in mind that electronic sources do have their limitations:

- not *all* published material is covered by the database you are using;
- nobody can find *all* the relevant material on a database;
- the full texts of the original articles are usually *not* available on bibliographic databases such as those offered by BIDS (although BIDS does provide a useful link to articles on its *JournalsOnline* Full Text Service).

If you wish to pursue the topic of database searching in greater detail, there is a guide:

> Cox, J. *et al.* (1997) *Key Guide to Information Sources in Online and CD-Rom Database Searching,* Mansell.

Table 4   Searching the ISI citation indexes, IBSS and Ei COMPENDEX via BIDS: some hints

Don't forget the online Help – click on the hypertext words or use the Help icon to find context-sensitive Help.

Searching
Use the 'Easy Search' form for straightforward author or subject searches; however, the 'Advanced Search' form draws attention to the many more options available

To change database or year range
Click in the box 'Using the ... database' to change to a different citation index or in one of the year boxes to change years (use your browser's 'Back' and 'Forward' buttons to move back and forth between screens); you have to go back to the BIDS home-page to change from IBSS Online to a citation index or vice versa.

To enter alternative words or phrases (Boolean operator: OR)
Type the words separated by a comma; so, for records which include *either* 'evaluation' *or* 'assessment':   **evaluation, assessment**

To require that both (or more) words or phrases be present (Boolean operator: AND)
Type the words separated by + or &; so, for records which include *both* 'evaluation' *and* 'marketing':   **evaluation+marketing**

To specify a phrase
Type in the phrase in the normal way – it will be read as a phrase: **marketing strategy**

To combine a number of operations
Use brackets to link combinations of keywords; e.g. to find *either* hospitals *or* nhs AND innovation *or* change.   **(nhs,hospitals) + (innovation, change)**

To look at the full record
For more detail when records are already displayed in a shortened format (e.g. title and author) click on the number to get the complete record.

To truncate or search using a 'wild card'
Use * to truncate; e.g. **market*** will find 'market' or 'markets' or 'marketing'.   **market***

To specify language or document type
Click on 'Advanced Search Form'; scroll down to the 'language(s)' box or the 'document type(s)' box and make your selections.

To reuse previous search sets
Click in 'Use Previous Searches' and combine the sets by using set numbers and BIDS symbols; so, to exclude from set 4 the results of search set 2, type **4-2**:   **4-2**

To save a search strategy (in order to run it again later)
Click on the 'Save/Retrieve Searches' and then on 'Save'; click in the box next to the search you wish to save and make a note of the 'identifier' that appears on the screen; to rerun the search at a later date, click on 'Save/Retrieve Searches', type the set identifier in the box, click on 'Retrieve' and follow instructions (note the 'since...date' box allows you to update your search).

To assemble a bibliography and transfer it to your own computer
'Check' the records you are interested in by clicking in the box by the record. You will not be able to receive them by e-mail until you 'mark' them too. To do this, select 'Mark Checked Articles' (*always do this before you move to the 'Next page'*). Then *either* 'E-mail Marked List' (the neatest solution) *or* 'Display Marked List' and use your browser to print or 'save' the references (save as a text file, e.g. inclusive.txt).

Table 5 Searching on OCLC FirstSearch: some hints

Don't forget the online Help.

Searching
Select the Advanced Search option – this indicates to you how to search more accurately and how to set up your search.

N.B. To avoid losing data, OCLC advise you to move between screens using the links and buttons on FirstSearch rather than your browser's Back, Forward, Stop, etc.

To enter alternative words or phrases (Boolean operator: OR)
– In Advanced Search, click the AND box & choose OR;
– You can also type **or** (but no more than two in any search) between the words: **innovation or creativity**

To require that two or more words or phrases be present (Boolean operator: AND)
– The Advanced Search form defaults to AND, so type your words in separate boxes;
– You can also type **and** between the words: **strategy and innovation**

To combine a number of operations
Use brackets to group terms together logically; e.g. to retrieve records that contain *either* innovation *or* creativity *and* design: **(innovation or creativity) and design**

To search a particular part of a record
Click on the 'Keyword Index' box in Basic Search, or on one of the 'Index' boxes in Advanced Search to see the available options, e.g. 'Subject Hdgs (Keyword)' to search by subject heading (subject headings are the terms used by the database indexers to describe the contents of the article).

To specify a phrase
Type the words separated by **w** (here the actual phrase 'knowledge management' appears, rather than the words occurring separately somewhere in the record):   **knowledge w management**

To specify that words should be adjacent in any order
Type **n** between the words – e.g. for 'Elisha McCoy' or 'McCoy, Elisha':   **elisha n mccoy**
a number (1–25) after **n/w** allows for intervening words, e.g. 'public sector utilities':   **public n1 utilities**

To include the plural of a word (this is the only 'truncation' or 'wild card' possible)
Type **+** at the end of the word; e.g. for 'model' or 'models' (but not 'modelling'):   **model+**

To reuse previous search results
Click on 'History'. It is now possible to combine previous search results (e.g. to exclude from your current set titles from a previous set which you have already looked through, tick in the boxes next to the two sets, and choose the 'connector' NOT; of course, you can also link them by choosing AND or OR).

To find ways of searching not shown on the screen
Click on the Help icon:
– For further advice on searching, click on 'General Help Topics'
– For information on the special fields (subject terms, author, publisher, etc.) which you can search on each database, click on Help and then on the specific database Help (e.g. 'WorldCat Database Help Topics') and select 'Labels'.

To limit by publication year, language, material type
Select the Advanced Search option and follow instructions.

Final output of results
'Tag' the records you are interested in (up to a maximum of 20). You must 'Save' tagged records *before* you move to another page or the tagging marks are erased. To receive records by e-mail, select 'Show' the tagged records and follow the instructions. (N.B. Any displayed record can be e-mailed to you individually.) Or, you can use your browser to print or save the list.

Before you start assembling another set of 20 records, you need to 'Clear' the tagged records you have just dealt with.

Table 6   Searching the *Business and Industry* Database via NISS: some hints

Don't forget the online Help – use the Help (question mark) icon.

Searching
Use the 'Advanced Search' form as, unlike the 'Simple Search' form, it enables you to search the whole archive (not just the last six months) and has many more options available.

To change the year and/or month range
Click in the box 'from year' and select the year from which your search will start, then click in the box 'to year' and select the year at which your search will end. The start and end months can be selected in a similar manner.

To enter alternative words or phrases (Boolean operator: OR)
The logical operator 'or' can be used where synonymous words or phrases are to be entered. The example opposite would retrieve records which include *either* 'advertising' *or* 'promotion':

    advertising or promotion

To require that both (or more) words or phrases be present (Boolean operator: AND)
You can type in 'and'; however, when more than one word is input, they are automatically (by default) 'anded' together. So, for records which include *both* 'emerging' *and* 'markets':

    emerging and markets
    or
    emerging markets

To specify a phrase
It is not possible to specify a phrase; e.g. 'emerging markets' is read as 'emerging and markets'.

To look at the full record
Click on the title of the article to view further bibliographic details and the full text (if it is available).

To truncate or search using a 'wild card'
Use * to truncate; e.g. **market*** will find 'market' or 'markets' or 'marketing':

    market*

To specify a region and/or industry term(s) to be searched
Click on 'Advanced Search'; scroll down to the 'Region' box and/or the 'Industry Term(s)' box and make your selections. *This is an important feature of the database.*

To sort the search results and specify the maximum number of articles to be retrieved
The order in which the article titles are sorted (including in order of relevance) can be specified. It is also possible to specify the maximum number of articles to be retrieved. Scroll down to the bottom of the advanced search form for these two options.

To transfer the information to your own computer
When you have the bibliographic details and/or full text on your screen, use your web browser to print or 'save' the information (save as a text file, e.g. emerge.txt).

> **Note**
> When the advanced search does not retrieve any articles, the screen prompts you to return to the form. Clicking on this link takes you to a different form (not the advanced search form that was first used) which does not have any links to the 'button bar'.

5.6.2 A selection of databases

Here is a small sample of databases. Details of many more can be found in the guides listed at the end of the section and in some of the specialized guides to information sources listed in Section 6.1.

Databases offered by more than one host or in different electronic formats will often differ in name or distribution of data between files, but the overall content will be essentially the same.

Through BIDS (Bath Information and Data Services), you have access to some valuable databases (for more detail, see the list that follows):

- *Ei Compendex* (technology)
- *IBSS* (International Bibliography of the Social Sciences)
- *Science Citation Index*
- *Social Sciences Citation Index*.

Through OCLC FirstSearch (Online Computer Library Center Inc.), you have access to many more databases, including:

- *ArticleFirst*
- *ContentsFirst* ('current contents')
- *PapersFirst* (conference papers)
- *Wilson Business Abstracts* (indexes over 300 periodicals)
- *WorldCat* (very large book catalogue).

Through NISS (National Information Services and Systems), you have access to:

- *Business and Industry* Database (extensive coverage of business and industry news)
- *EBSCO MasterFile*.

As well as the general remarks above (Section 5.6.1) on searching computer databases and the hints on searching BIDS, OCLC FirstSearch, and *Business and Industry* Database, you will find examples of straightforward searches in the Case Study (Section 8).

We have put a 'core five' at the beginning: *if you want to find references to journal articles or books on a subject, it will probably be enough just to look at one or two of these.* However, in case you want to look further, we have listed several more that might be useful, particularly those available free to OU students or issued in CD-Rom format. We have also indicated which CD-Roms can be found at the Business Information Service (BIS) in the Science Reference and Information Service (SRIS), 25 Southampton Building, London WC2A 1AW (0171–323 7457, or to book slots for searching business CD-Roms, 0171–412 7454).

Moreover, many CD-Roms are now being provided by the larger public libraries. The policy of university and other non-public libraries towards granting outsiders access to electronic sources varies widely. Some will allow you access to BIDS if you use your OU passwords, some not. Some will allow you to use their CD-Roms, some not. So, it might well be worthwhile having a chat with librarians in your area to find out what is possible for you locally.

Indexes of journal articles, books and reports

A core five

ABI/INFORM (UMI)

Abstracts of articles from 800 business and management journals; useful and comprehensive: the full text of some articles is available online.

CD-Rom (available at BIS/SRIS).

Business and Industry Database (Responsive Database Services Inc.)

Covers 880 trade and business periodicals drawn from 33 different countries; world wide coverage of a broad range of industries; 60% of the records provide the full text of articles. New records are added daily. This database is particularly useful because it can be searched by geographic region and by industry term.

Via NISS: free for OU students

Internet access – http://niss.ac.uk/b+i/

Social Sciences Citation Index (ISI)

Title, keyword and citation searching (see Section 5.6.1) of 1,400 journals. Provides links to any complete articles which are available on BIDS JournalsOnline (Section 5.3).

BIDS: free to OU students
CD-Rom.

Wilson Business Abstracts (H.W. Wilson)

Indexes and abstracts articles from 340 business magazines in accounting, advertising, finance, personnel, small business, etc.

OCLC FirstSearch: free to OU students
CD-Rom

WorldCat (OCLC)

More than 36,000,000 records of books and AV material catalogued by OCLC member libraries; very useful for tracing books.

OCLC FirstSearch: free to OU students

Other indexes: General

ArticleFirst (OCLC)

Index to 12,500 journals in science, technology, medicine, social science and business; 1990–on.

OCLC FirstSearch: free to OU students

ContentsFirst (OCLC)

Complete table-of-contents pages of 12,500 journals; useful for checking the contents of journals that interest you but which you do not have to hand; very up-to-date; 1990–on.

OCLC FirstSearch: free to OU students

SIGLE (SilverPlatter)

System for Information on Grey Literature in Europe; useful for difficult-to-trace papers, pamphlets, theses and translations from government, local government, universities and learned societies; all documents available from the British Library's Document Supply Centre.

CD-Rom (available at BIS/SRIS)

UnCover (Blackwell's and CARL Systems Inc.)

Index to 5,000,000 articles from 15,000 journals in many fields; online ordering of original articles possible, at a cost of about $14 per article faxed.

Internet access – http://uncweb.carl.org

Business and management

ABI/INFORM (UMI)

See under 'A core five' above.

Anbar Electronic Intelligence (MCB University Press)

Equivalent to the printed abstracts: *Accounting and Finance, Information Management and Technology, Marketing and Distribution, Operations and Production Management, Personnel and Training* and *Top Management*; abstracts are 'quality-graded'.

CD-Rom

Business and Industry Database

See under 'A core five' above.

F and S Indexes Plus Text (Information Access Company/Silver Platter)

F and S Indexes and *Predicasts Overview of Markets and Technology*; multi-industry, international coverage of companies, products, markets and applied technologies; abstracts and figures (and some full texts) taken from journals, newspapers, newsletters, research studies, analysts' reports and company press releases and annual reports.

CD-Rom (available at BIS/SRIS)

FAME (Bureau van Dijk and Jordans)

Financial data from Companies House on 100,000 companies, plus 30 business ratios. Analytical and graphics capabilities enable you to compare a given company's financial variables with its industry norms or with its individual competitors; statistical analysis also offered. Other CDs cover Europe (*AMADEUS*) and Japan (*JADE*).

CD-Rom (available at BIS/SRIS)

Institute of Management International Databases Plus

Abstracts of journal articles, books, management working papers, company practice policy documents and audio-visual material held in the Institute's library.

CD-Rom (free searching for Institute members, with photocopy and loan services – see entry in Section 7.2)

Wilson Business Abstracts

See under 'A core five' above.

Social sciences

BHI Plus (Bowker-Saur)

Equivalent to the printed *British Humanities Index*. Indexes 320 journals and newspapers. Coverage includes some business topics, current affairs, economics and the environment.

CD-Rom

IBSS ONLINE (British Library of Political and Economic Science)

Important source in the social sciences. Equivalent to the printed *International Bibliography of the Social Sciences*. Indexes 2,600 journals, lists 6,000 books a year and indexes chapters of multi-authored books. 1950–on. Provides links to any complete articles which are available on BIDS JournalsOnline (Section 5.3).

BIDS: free to OU students

Social Sciences Citation Index

See under 'A core five' above.

Technology

ANTE PLUS (Bowker-Saur)

Abstracts in New Technologies and Engineering and *CATNI (Catchword and Trade Name Index);* covers 320 UK and US journals; useful for quickly finding material on technology developments and on companies and new products.

CD-Rom

Ei Compendex / Page One (Engineering Information Inc.)

Compendex has abstracts of journal articles, reports and conference papers in 2,600 international publications, covering technology in its broadest sense. *Ei Page One* indexes 5,400 journals and also technical reports, book chapters, etc., but has no abstracts. Provides links to any complete articles which are available on BIDS JournalsOnline (Section 5.3).

BIDS: free to OU students
CD-Rom (available at BIS/SRIS)

Microcomputer Abstracts (Learned Information Inc.)

More than 75 popular magazines and professional journals on microcomputing in business, education and the home; news, articles, reviews, new products, software evaluations.

OCLC FirstSearch: free to OU students

Recent Advances in Manufacturing (RAM)

Abstracts of articles from 500 journals, plus details of books, conference proceedings, etc. Available on a trial basis via EEVL (see 5.3).

Internet access – http://www.eevl.ac.uk

Science Citation Index (ISI)

Title, keyword and citation searching (see Section 5.6.1) of 4,400 journals in science and technology. Provides links to any complete articles which are available on BIDS JournalsOnline (Section 5.3).

BIDS: free to OU students
CD-Rom (available at BIS/SRIS)

Indexes to conference proceedings

PapersFirst (OCLC/British Library)

Index of the 500,000 conference papers received at the British Library's Document Supply Centre each year; October 1993–on.

OCLC FirstSearch: free to OU students
CD-Rom (*Inside Conferences* – available at BIS/SRIS)

> *ProceedingsFirst* (OCLC/British Library)
>
> Entries for all the conferences received at the British Library's Document Supply Centre since October 1993.
>
> OCLC FirstSearch: free to OU students
> CD-Rom (*Inside Conferences* – available at BIS/SRIS)

Full texts

For information about electronic access to the full texts of **newspapers**, see 'Newspapers online' in Section 5.4, Newspapers.

For information on electronic **journals**, see 'Journals online' in Section 5.3, Journals – printed and online.

Market and stockbroker reports

The full texts of reports from sources such as the following are offered (at a price) by FT Profile and others:

> Euromonitor;
>
> ICC;
>
> Henley Centre;
>
> Mintel;
>
> stockbrokers;
>
> *Financial Times Newsletters*.

CD-Roms you might come across are:

> *InvesText* (Information Access Company)
>
> 30,000 full text reports from companies worldwide and stockbroking, banking and research firms.
>
> CD-Rom (available at BIS/SRIS)

> *UK Company Factfinder* (Knight-Ridder Information)
>
> Financial data covering 10 years, and full text reports from companies and from investment, marketing and finance analysts; covers all companies quoted on the Stock Exchange.
>
> CD-Rom (available at BIS/SRIS)

Company directories

KOMPASS CD Book (Reed Information Services)

50,000 UK companies; access to the contents of *KOMPASS* volumes 1 and 2; 41,000 product categories.

CD-Rom

Statistics and datasets (see also Section 6.5)

BIRON (Economic and Social Research Council)

Detailed indexes of the datasets in the Data Archive of the Economic and Social Research Council.

Internet access – http://dawww.essex.ac.uk

FactSearch (Pierian Press Inc.)

Facts and statistics from some 300 works, including newspapers, periodicals, the Congressional Record and congressional hearings. Abstracts of articles with figures (not time series).

OCLC FirstSearch: free to OU students

International Statistical Yearbook (Data Service and Information)

600,000 time series from EU/Eurostat, OECD, IMF, UNIDO, CITICORP, etc.

CD-Rom

OECD Statistical Compendium (Data Service and Information)

220,000 time series (1960–on), covering food, agriculture, economic indicators, national accounts, energy, industry, science and technology, etc.

CD-Rom

Many useful recent statistics and economic indicators are available via the following URL:

http://www.oecd.org/statlist.htm

Quest Economics (Janet Matthews Information Services/Chadwyck-Healey)

1,000 country reports, plus statistics and economic data, forecasts and analysis from research departments, banks, etc.

CD-Rom (available at BIS/SRIS)

Statistical Masterfile (Congressional Information Service)

Index of statistical series; combines *American Statistics Index* (US official), *Statistical Reference Index* (American non-official) and *Index to International Statistics* (series from international bodies).

CD–Rom

World Marketing Data and Statistics (Euromonitor)

Equivalent to the printed *European Marketing Data and Statistics* and *International Marketing Data and Statistics*.

CD-Rom

Book and library catalogues (see also Sections 4 and 5.1)

COPAC (Consortium of University Research Libraries)

One-stop access to several important university library catalogues.

Internet access – http://copac.ac.uk/copac/

Internet Book Shop

More than 1 million books in print in the UK; at the opening screen, click on 'Search'; books can ordered online.

Internet access – http://www.bookshop.co.uk/

OPAC 97 (British Library)

BL Catalogue 1450–1975, Science Reference & Information Service Catalogue 1976–on, Science, Technology & Business Current Catalogue, Document Supply Centre Catalogues. etc.

Internet access – http://opac97.bl.uk/

> *University Library Catalogues*
>
> Access to all the catalogues (separately) via the NISS Information Gateway.
>
> Internet access – http://www.niss.ac.uk →Reference →Library OPACS ...

> *WorldCat*
>
> See under 'A core five' above.

Guides to CD-Roms and online databases

> Allcock, S. and Whitby, L. (1996) *The Online Manual: Practical Guide to Business Databases,* 6th edn, Learned Information.
>
> Armstrong, C. J. (1995) *World Databases in Management,* Bowker-Saur.
>
> English, L. (1994) *CD-Rom and Online Business and Company Databases,* 4th edn, Aslib.
>
> *CD-Rom Directory with Multimedia CDs,* annual, TFPL Publishing.
>
> *CD-Roms in Print,* annual, Mecklermedia.
>
> *Gale Directory of Databases* (1997) 2 volumes, Gale Research (online, CD-Rom, diskette, etc.).
>
> *Online/CD-Rom Business Sourcebook,* annual, Headland Business Information.
>
> *The Prentice Hall Directory of Online Business Information 1996–1997; with CD-Rom* (1996) Prentice Hall.

There is a useful catalogue issued by a commercial supplier of CD-Roms:

> *Microinfo CD-Rom Catalogue,* Microinfo Ltd. (PO Box 3, Omega Park, Alton, Hampshire GU34 2PG).

Finally, some of the guides to information sources (Section 6.1) cover databases, and Aslib, of 20–24 Old Street, London EC1V 9AP (0171–253 4488) will give advice on all aspects of online usage (a fee will be charged for non-members).

5.6.3 The Internet

The databases discussed above are well known and systematically organized. However, the thousands of computers connected to the Internet represent potentially vast information resources. Older methods of communication between computers, such as Telnet, although still utilized, have been superseded by the World Wide Web. This provides a way of finding your way around the system. Clicking on 'hypermedia' links (highlighted or underlined names, phrases or images) enables the user to move from one 'page' to another. Behind the highlighted link there is an address. Your (the 'client's') software (Netscape, say) calls up the relevant page from the information provider's computer ('server').

Sources may include information about organizations, product catalogues, the full text of research reports, details of special interest discussion groups (which you can join), graphics, video and so on. Each location on the Internet has its own unique address or URL (Uniform Resource Locator). These are the http:// tags that appear throughout this Guide.

We shall not go into any detail here about the general use of the Internet (see below for remarks on using the Internet as a source of information), but here are three points for the beginner:

- Use your browser's 'Back' button to retrace your steps screen by screen – very useful if you take a wrong turning.
- Use the 'Bookmark' facility (in Netscape) or 'Favorites' (in Microsoft Internet Explorer) to save time and have a record of useful sites (e.g. click on 'Bookmark' and then on 'Add Bookmark' – the next time you click on 'Bookmark', you will see the site name and need only click there to make the connection).
- Wherever you are during an Internet session, look for online 'Help' if you run into difficulty.

There are online courses available on the Internet itself (see below). Particularly recommended is the material at the Netskills site. To access this:

1 Open Netscape (or other Internet browser) by clicking on its icon.
2 In the 'Location' (URL) box type

   http://www.netskills.ac.uk/TONIC/

Some printed guides are given below – Winship's is a useful starting-point.

Evaluating web resources

Warning: the quality of what you find on the Internet varies just as widely (or even more so) as the quality of printed material. So, think first in the same sort of terms as you would when assessing the value of a book or journal article, and then you might consider some web-type criteria:

- What is the authority of the author or sponsoring body?
- Is the information up-to-date?
- Is the material controlled, refereed (e.g. assessed by fellow academics) or checked in some way? (If a site is found through the gateways discussed below, that in itself indicates that some evaluation has taken place.)
- Does the information seem objective? Or is there an underlying marketing or propaganda motive?

And, less importantly, from the web point of view:

- Is there a clear structure to the pages? Is the presentation clear? Is there online help and guidance? Can you get through to the site reliably and quickly?

>Note that many Internet sites provide contact points to enable you to make your own comments and suggestions about the site.

Search method

There are detailed notes on 'Searching databases' in Section 5.6.1: bear in mind when searching the Internet that *the same general principles apply*. There are many reasons why a search on the Internet can fail:

- most obviously, the information sought is not there (try a library!)
- faulty or busy communication links (quite common – it is often worth trying again later)
- the vast and unstructured nature of the system (see below for palliatives)

but a very common reason is

- faulty search technique.

So, remember it is important to:

- choose the right keywords (use your imagination)
- combine keywords logically (look again at steps 14 and 15 in Section 5.6.1).

If you find a mass of unpromising material, think in terms of the Boolean AND: "I don't want every mention of 'wind', only those where, say, 'turbines' are mentioned" (or 'renewable', or whatever). You will almost always be able to search like that, typing in the search box something like **wind and turbines**.

So, *think in Boolean terms* and *look for online Help* on expressing a search precisely.

Search engines and gateways

There are two main approaches to searching for information on the Internet:

- using *search engines*
- using *gateways* (or 'directories' or 'catalogues').

A search engine ranges across the web looking for sites which mention your search words. Gateways or directories select sites and arrange them in a more or less structured way, making a search more like searching for books in a library where material is classified and shelved in a systematic way.

Table 7 The Internet: search engines and gateways

	Advantages	Disadvantages
Search engines	– can search millions of pages – worldwide scope – easy to use	– much of what is found is dross – sites are searched at random (rather than searching a 'Technology' set) – sites not described properly – often American-oriented – sometimes the links do not work
Gateways	– sites have been evaluated – sites structured in a way that allows fruitful browsing (like a library) – often tailored for particular audiences (e.g. EEVL) and therefore more likely to be relevant – links regularly tested	– very small selection of what is on the Internet – dependent on other people's decisions and judgements – loses the freewheeling, anarchic quality of the Internet

These categories are not completely clear-cut: some of the search engines incorporate reviewing and some of the gateways, e.g. EEVL, allow you to search not only the pages of the sites directly on the system, but also the pages on the sites to which the 'EEVL sites' provide links (to five levels).

Examples of **search engines** are Alta Vista, Excite, HotBot, Inference Find, Infoseek and Lycos.

> http://www.altavista.telia.com/
> http://www.excite.com/
> http://www.hotbot.com/
> http://m5.inference.com/ifind/
> http://www.infoseek.com/
> http://www-uk.lycos.com/

The search engines vary a great deal in method and what they retrieve. If you find you use them a lot, work out which are best for your purposes. Look at factors such as

- speed
- number of hits
- quality of information provided on the sites found.

A new category, 'meta' searchers, activates a group of search engines. For example, the 'metacrawler' runs a search over five search engines and presents the results as a combined set:

> http://www.metacrawler.com/

'Megaweb' also searches simultaneously over several search engines, and returns a complete set of results.

> http://stoat.shef.ac.uk:8080/megaweb/

The OU itself, in its web pages, provides not only its own material, but also acts as a **gateway** to other Internet resources. For example, the OU Library's web pages are designed to provide a structured way of accessing this mass of material. You will find routes to some of the information resources mentioned in this Guide, such as bibliographic databases, online journals and university library catalogues, and also links to other gateways, a guide to the Internet and 'search engines', and links to training materials on databases and the Internet. To reach them go to:

> http://oulib1.open.ac.uk/lib/

The NISS Information Gateway is a useful starting-point to have bookmarked for accessing databases such as those on BIDS, OCLC FirstSearch, Business and Industry Database, and the EBSCO MasterFILE (click on 'External Data Services'), university library catalogues (click on 'Reference', then 'Library OPACs'), and newspapers (click on 'News'):

> http://www.niss.ac.uk/

Starting at NISS's 'External Data Services', OU students can access a database of standardized descriptions of web sites called *NetFirst*. At *NetFirst*'s opening screen, enter your search in the form provided. You can specify the Dewey decimal classification numbers found in libraries as well as keywords; for example, you can ask for records where the word 'quality' is mentioned and which are classified in the Dewey 650s (covering management). The system responds with a list of site titles arranged in Dewey order. Click on a site title and the standard description comes up including a summary, site contacts, classification numbers, and so on. If the site still sounds interesting, click on the hypertext site title to get through to it. Passwords are needed – see the beginning of Section 5.6 for general information on gaining access to these protected databases.

A structured gateway that allows for browsing over a wide range of subjects is

The BUBL Information Service (click on 'BUBL Link: the Subject Tree'):

> http://bubl.ac.uk/

Business and management gateways

Top of the list of specialized business information gateways for UK users of the Internet are Biz/ed and Sheila Webber's 'Business Information Sources on the Internet'.

Supported by both education and industry, **Biz/ed** is a gateway to quality-assessed business and economics information on the Internet. It provides 'company facts' for a limited number of companies; economics, business and finance data sets for the UK and overseas, and a regularly updated Listings section which is essentially a searchable and 'browsable' Internet resources catalogue. The Listings section indexes over 500 resources which have been selected and described by subject specialists. The Biz/ed site is easy to navigate, and downloads quickly.

> http://bized.ac.uk/

Sheila Webber's *Business Information Sources on the Internet* provides a searchable guide to approximately 450 selected business information sources on the Internet. Selection criteria include: coverage, currency and reliability. The links are updated and validated regularly. Coverage is world-wide, with an emphasis on Europe (particularly the UK). This site is indexed by subject area, including:

- company directories
- company profiles and financial information
- country information
- statistical, economic and market information
- news sources.

Sheila Webber's site also provides a useful index of other guides to Internet sites with business information.

> http://www.dis.strath.ac.uk/business/index.html

There are several other useful business and management gateways and many Internet sites which provide business and management information. A few of these are listed (with descriptions) below.

B*net*: **Business on the Internet** is run by Frontal Limited, in conjunction with the Department of Trade and Industry. Bnet is up-dated daily, and provides access to information which is, in the main, produced by government departments, professional bodies and leading commercial organizations. These include: the DTI, the CBI and Arthur Andersen. Subscription to Bnet is free to all students. After you have completed and submitted a form you will receive (by e-mail) an initial username and password.

Subjects covered by Bnet include: Finance, Administrative Management, Human Resources, Business Services, Innovation & Research, Purchasing

& Supply, Sales, Manufacturing, Marketing and International Trade. Management guides, directories, case studies, abstracts, extracts and events details are available within each subject area.

http://www.bnet.co.uk/

BizInfo: A guide to conducting business research on the Internet is maintained by the Harvard Business School. Lists of web sites (with descriptions) are categorized under headings which include: company profiles; company directories; stock quotes; government information and patents. The links within BizInfo are tested on a bimonthly basis.

http://www.hbs.edu/applegate/bizinfo3/

BRINT: A Business Researchers Interests, a searchable site, is edited and published by Yogesh Malhotra of the University of Pittsburgh. Lists of links to sites are provided under various headings, which include: Business and technology (from which you can find links to company and business information sources); International business and technology; Business process reengineering and innovation; and Knowledge management and organizational learning.

http://www.brint.com/interest.html

A Business Compass abstracts and indexes selected business information sources on the Internet. The site is searchable and browsable under broad subject headings.

http://www.abcompass.com/home.html

The **Business Webliography** provides an annotated listing of Internet resources in several subject areas, including business and management. It is maintained by librarians and staff of Louisiana State University Libraries. Subjects covered include: Accounting, Business and Industry News, Economics and Statistics, and Management and Entrepreneurship.

http://www.lib.lsu.edu/weblio.html#Business/

The **Enterprise Zone** is backed by the UK Government. It is searchable and provides links to information, resources, and sources of expertise on marketing, business legislation and regulations, and information technology. All sites indexed by this service have been evaluated using the following criteria: Quality, Authority, Stability, Objectivity, Currency, Usability, Accuracy and Coverage.

http://www.enterprisezone.org.uk/

The **Harvard Business School's Baker Library** acts as a gateway to business and management resources on the Internet; the company and industry information sections are particularly useful.

http://library.hbs.edu/

International Business Resources on the WWW is maintained by Michigan State University and provides a searchable index of international business resources.

http://ciber.bus.msu.edu/busres.htm

Other gateways

Information resources of relevance to business and management are also accessible via gateways in other specific subject areas, such as technology and social sciences.

EEVL is a gateway administered for UK higher education to cover the broad field of technology. It is possible to limit your search to commercial servers.

http://www.eevl.ac.uk/

You can expand outwards from the UK by making use of the **Ei Village** as a whole. At the opening page you will see a 'map' of icons corresponding to the categories above, leading to 16,000 sites and services. Get to the Ei Village either through the NISS gateway (http://www.niss.ac.uk – click on 'Subscription services') or go direct to:

http://www.ei-village.org.uk/village/

The Ei Village maintains the British Engineering Centre in conjunction with EEVL. The Centre covers:
- Business & Financial District (business news and links)
- Industry Mart (product catalogues, etc.)
- Library
- Government Centre
- and more.

SOSIG (Social Science Information Gateway) describes and links to network resources in subject areas including: economics, development, management, accountancy and business.

http://sosig.ac.uk/

Resources for economists on the Internet has been created by Bill Goffe, an economist at the University of Southern Mississippi. This site lists links to Internet resources in the field of economics.

http://econwpa.wustl.edu/EconFAQ/EconFAQ.html

NetEc exists to improve the communication of research in Economics via electronic media. The NetEc site provides links to information resources in economics, including BibEc, through which the bibliographic details of printed working papers can be accessed (free of charge).

http://netec.mcc.ac.uk/NetEc.html

Discussion lists

A discussion list is comprised of a group of people who share a common interest in the discussion topic and exchange messages via e-mail. Discussion lists are also termed 'mailing lists' and 'electronic conferences'. Members are often discussing recent issues, networking, organizing meetings and helping each other with queries. You usually need to join a discussion list before you can participate. Please note that some lists are not publicly accessible. It is worth finding out which topics are covered before joining a list. In addition to viewing the list's access, joining and coverage information it is often possible to search its archives. You may find that a particular topic of interest has already been discussed.

There are several directories of discussion lists, including **Liszt** and **Mailbase**.

Liszt is a searchable discussion list directory which can also be browsed by subject. Many business related lists, which cover subjects including 'ethics', 'marketing' and 'technology', can be accessed via the 'business' subject heading.

> http://www.liszt.com/

The Mailbase lists can be searched, or browsed, either by subject category, or alphabetically by list name. There are many business and management related lists under the 'Social Sciences' subject heading.

> http://www.mailbase.ac.uk

Courses and books about the Internet

Online courses on the Internet and its use include:

Netskills's *Tonic* (particularly recommended)

> http://www.netskills.ac.uk/TONIC/

Walt Howe's Internet Learning Center

> http://world.std.com/~walthowe/

There are useful surveys of Internet resources and search engines:

> Tillman, H.N. (1997) *Evaluating quality on the Net* [online], http://www.tiac.net/users/hope/findqual.html [site accessed: September, 1997].

> Tyner, R. (1997) *Sink or swim: Internet search tools and techniques* [online]. Available from: Okanagan University College, British Columbia, Canada, http://www.sci.ouc.bc.ca/libr/connect96/search.htm [site accessed: September, 1997].

There are some helpful books:

> Krol, E. (1996) *The Whole Internet User's Guide and Catalog,* Academic Edition, Integra Media Group/O'Reilly;

> Winship, I. and McNab, A. (1996) *The Student's Guide to the Internet,* Library Association Publishing.

UK sources are covered by:

> Pope, I. (1995) *Internet UK,* Prentice Hall.

Finally, keep your eye on the journals. Surveys of Internet resources frequently appear.

6 SOURCES OF INFORMATION: SPECIALIZED AREAS

In Section 5 we covered what we called 'the basics'. However, there are many specialized areas of information which you might want to look at from time to time. Section 6 starts with a reminder that many long and detailed guides to business and management information exist, and continues with brief overviews of the 'The UK government and its publications', 'Standards', 'Patents', the important area of 'Statistics and market data', ' Trade literature and product data', 'Reports', 'Conference papers' and 'Theses'.

6.1 GUIDES TO INFORMATION SOURCES, SUBJECT BIBLIOGRAPHIES

There are many specialized guides that aim to give an overview of sources of information in their fields. If you have a particularly difficult information problem, you might well find an answer in one of the following guides:

Business Information Basics, annual, Headland Business Information;

The Business Library and How to Use It: A Guide to Sources and Research Strategies for Information on Business and Management (1996) Omnigraphics;

Croner's A–Z of Business Information Sources, Croner Publications (loose-leaf with updating service);

Mort, D. (ed.) (1997) *Market Research Sourcebook,* Headland Business Information;

Pagell, R. A. et al. (1994) *International Business Information: How to Find It, How to Use It,* Oryx Press;

Sources of European Economic and Business Information (1995) 6th edn, Gower (British Library Business Information Research Service)

Spencer, N. (1995) *How to Find Information – Business: A Guide to Searching in Published Sources*, British Library;

Tudor, J. (1992) *Macmillan Directory of UK Business Information Sources*, 3rd edn, Macmillan;

Woy, J. B. (editor) (1996) *Encyclopedia of Business Information Sources,* 11th edn, Gale Research.

Subject bibliographies (that is, lists of books and journal articles on a particular subject) can save a lot of time and trouble in searching, and one useful book or article traced this way may in its turn lead to more useful titles. Examples are:

Avery, C. and Zabel, D. (eds) (1996) *The Quality Management Sourcebook: an International Guide to Materials and Resources,* Routledge;

Encyclopedia of Business Information Sources: A Bibliographic Guide to more than 28,000 Citations Covering over 1,100 Subjects of Interest to Business Personnel, 1997–98 (1996) 11th edn, Gale Research.

Useful bibliographies may appear in journals. For example:

> Dahlgaard, J. J. *et al.* (1994) 'The quality journey', *Total Quality Management,* vol. 5, no. 1–2, pp. 1–160 (includes extensive bibliography).

Professional bodies may also issue bibliographies, such as:

> the Institute of Management's *Reading Lists for Management*

and you might come across the journal:

> *Management Bibliographies & Reviews,* 8 a year, Anbar Electronic Intelligence.

Bibliographies can also be found on the Internet. For example, the Baker Library of the Harvard Business School offers 'Reference Bibliographies' on a wide range of subjects:

> http://library.hbs.edu/refguide.htm

Tracing bibliographies

Subject bibliographies in both books and journals are indexed in:

> *Bibliographic Index,* H.W. Wilson, quarterly, annual cumulations.

Otherwise, trace bibliographies through the usual sources for tracing books (Section 5.1) or look in the abstracts and indexes (5.2). There might be a separate list of bibliographies or a subheading 'bibliographies' under the topic you are interested in. If you have access to online sources (Section 5.6), then you could look at the vast *WorldCat* database on OCLC FirstSearch – just type in 'bibliography' or 'bibliographies' and link that to a suitable subject keyword. Some organizations make bibliographies available over the Internet (see above and Section 5.6.3).

6.2 THE UK GOVERNMENT AND ITS PUBLICATIONS

Apart from the direct effects of the government's political, economic and spending activities, it is also an important collector and disseminator of business and statistical information. This section is meant to give you a brief introduction to the government's publications. Statistics are covered in Section 6.5. Some notes on government departments and some addresses are given in Section 7.

The pattern of government publishing is complicated. We shall not go into detail here about parliamentary and non-parliamentary papers, sessional papers, blue, green and white papers, and so on. However, these distinctions affect the ways in which different libraries deal with their government publications, so if you run into difficulties, ask a librarian for help. It is also important to be accurate when citing a government document. In tracing a document the following items can all be essential:

> name of the Ministry;

> date of publication or of the parliamentary session;

> any special numbers or letters, brackets, or whatever (for example, the abbreviation 'Cmd. 461' does not refer to the same report as 'Cmnd. 461').

Government (that is, Parliament, Ministers and the Civil Service) may respond to an issue in various ways:
- Members of Parliament may debate an issue. Debates are fully reported in *Hansard* (daily, weekly and bound volumes: there are good indexes to the weekly parts and the bound volumes; also available on CD-Rom);
- Questions, for oral and written reply, may be asked in Parliament. The written answers are often a useful source of information. They appear at the back of each daily part of *Hansard* and have a different, italicized sequence of column numbers;
- Committees may consider an issue:
    they might be specially appointed to *inquire* into the circumstances leading to a particular event or into a particular problem (for example, the Alvey Committee, whose influential report *A Programme for Advanced Information Technology* was published in 1982),
    they might sit as standing committees to *advise* on policy (e.g. Advisory Council on Science and Technology),
    or a Parliamentary Select Committee might turn its attention to an issue (for instance, the House of Lords Select Committee on Science and Technology, or one of the House of Commons Select Committees that oversee the activities of individual government departments, such as Trade and Industry and Environment).
- Committee reports may be based on a mass of evidence and research, which is often available in some form:
    as part of the report itself,
    as separately published appendices or House of Commons Papers,
    in a publication of the body submitting the evidence or doing the research.
- Finally, Ministerial thinking is outlined in 'White' or 'Green' (consultative) Papers.

The most important Ministry as far as business is concerned is the Department of Trade and Industry. The Department deals with:

consumer protection;

use of technology;

trade;

regional development;

industrial production;

monopoly matters;

small businesses.

It issues significant series of reports, such as the *Energy Papers*. Located within the Department is the Office of Science and Technology which administers the Technology Foresight programme and has issued 15 sector reports, *Progress through Partnership*, on the future of research and development in the UK.

Other important departments are the Department for Education and Employment, the Department of the Environment, Transport and the Regions etc..

Access to the web pages of government departments and offices is via the main government site (click on the 'Organizational' or 'Functional' indexes):

http://www.open.gov.uk/

Addresses of important ministries, and of the government's Regional Offices, are given in Section 7.

Tracing official publications

If you wish to trace a government document, the first place to look is in the various lists issued by The Stationery Office (previously Her Majesty's Stationery Office, HMSO, which continues to publish Acts of Parliament and Statutory Instruments). These are published daily, monthly, annually and on CD-Rom (ask about them at the library desk). The *Daily List* is also available on the Stationery Office web site – see below.

'Sectional Lists' show the titles of in-print publications on particular subjects. They are free: apply to The Stationery Office Books Marketing and Promotion, St. Crispin's, Duke Street, Norwich NR3 IPD (01603 695907) or look at their web site (see below). They include:

Sectional List No. 3: Energy, Trade and Industry;

Sectional List No. 5: Environment;

Sectional List No. 11: Health and Social Security;

Sectional List No. 22: Transport.

Many Ministries produce their own catalogues. The Department of Trade and Industry's is available free from their Library and Information Centre, Room LGD42, 1 Victoria Street, London SW1H 0ET (0171 215 6024).

Very good coverage of official publications is provided by the Internet site *BOPCAS: British Official Publications Current Awareness Service* (previously *NUKOP Online*). It provides update lists (including 'Economy', 'Europe', 'Statistics'; etc.); some reports may be browsed in full text and there are subject-based e-mail lists, where details of new publications in various fields are e-mailed to group members.

http://www.soton.ac.uk/~bopcas/

One of the best places to look is the professional and trade press which tries to keep readers informed of current government reports and policies. Since policies that affect business are frequently changing, it can be well worthwhile to keep an eye on one or two appropriate journals.

Many official reports are referred to by the name of the person who chaired the committee which produced them (*The Finniston report,* for example) and there are indexes to these. Ask your librarian if you have any query of this sort.

Names and addresses of Stationery Office book shops and agents are given in the Sectional Lists, and you might also look in the Yellow Pages. General enquiries about publications can be made to 0171–873 0011. Orders can be made directly on 0171–873 9090 or to Publications Centre, 51 Nine Elms Lane, London SW8 5DR. For non-Stationery Office publications, you can telephone 0171–873 8372. The Stationery Office home page on the Internet is:

http://www.the-stationery-office.co.uk/

where you can find the *Daily List*, the Sectional Lists mentioned above and the full texts of a few reports.

References to recent official reports, press releases, and in some cases full texts, can be found via the government:

http://www.open.gov.uk/

In general, the Library or Publicity Department of the appropriate Ministry or unit will be able to help with advice on publications and their availability, information on government policy, and so on.

6.3 STANDARDS

Standards embody accepted current methodologies and technologies, relating, for example, to quality, testing, terminology and codes of practice. Apart from their importance to the designer, they also have obvious commercial importance. It is often vital to investigate relevant standards at an early stage of product development, since they may be the means through which a client or regulatory body (perhaps in a foreign market) expresses certain minimum standards that are legally or contractually required. Observing such standards from the outset may avoid the need to make expensive alterations later.

Detailed guidance to the series of standards dealing with quality systems, *BS EN ISO 9000–9004* (previously known as *BS 5750*), is provided by the QMH 100 handbook:

> *QMH 100: 1995: Quality Management Handbook. Part 1: Quality Assurance: Part 2: 1992: Reliability and Maintainability* (contains the full text of some of the most important quality-related standards).

The International Organization for Standardization (ISO) issues a compendium:

> *ISO 9000 Quality Management Compendium* (1996) 6th edn, ISO.

The increasingly important field of environmental control is covered by:

> *BS 7750: 1994: Specification for Environmental Management Systems*;
>
> *ISO 14000* standards (now being developed by the International Standards Organization: still in draft form at the time of writing, but see below for the ISO Internet pages),

and the 'Year 2000 Problem' is dealt with in:

> *DISC PD2000-1, A Definition of Year 2000 Conformity Requirements*.

Tracing standards

The central standardizing body in the UK is the **British Standards Institution (BSI)**, at 389 Chiswick High Road, London W4 4AL. The Library maintains a reference collection of British and foreign national standards, and overseas laws, regulations and other standards and technical requirements, together with indexes. An Information Centre (0181–996 7111) will answer any question relating to standards, including foreign standards. These often present particular problems, since, as in the USA, they may be issued by literally hundreds of different bodies, public and private. The BSI Sales Department also deals with both British and foreign standards.

The annual *BSI Standards Catalogue* lists the libraries that hold complete sets of British Standards. Full sets of standards on microfiche published by Technical Indexes Ltd. are widely found. Otherwise, look in specialized directories (Sections 5.1, 6.6, 7.1) and handbooks, which often list relevant standards and codes of practice, or contact organizations, particularly trade and research associations (Section 5.5). Trade journals outline and comment on them, often while they are still in draft form.

ISO On-line offers free access via the World Wide Web on the Internet to the International Standards Organization Catalogue. Bibliographic references to the standards are searchable via a hierarchical classification scheme. The standards themselves can then be obtained from the BSI (Customer Services: 0181–996 7000). Also available is general information on the ISO and facts on the ISO 9000 Forum, which supports implementation of the ISO 9000 quality management standards. The URL (Internet) address is:

http://www.iso.ch/welcome.html

6.4 PATENTS

We shall not go into detail about the nature of patents. Apart from their obvious commercial significance, they can be a valuable source of up-to-date and unique technological information but they present many difficulties for the inexperienced user. If you have a problem involving patents, consult British Library Patents Information, Science Reference and Information Service, 25 Southampton Buildings, London WC2A 1AW (general patent enquiries: 0171–412 7919/20) or go to one of the regional participants in the Patents Information Network situated in the central libraries of Aberdeen, Belfast, Birmingham, Bristol, Coventry, Glasgow, Leeds, Liverpool, Manchester, Newcastle-upon-Tyne, Plymouth, Portsmouth and Sheffield.

Patents on the Internet

The best sources on the Internet are American, but they still provide a good entry-point.

IBM offers an excellent free service covering US patent descriptions back to 1971:

http://patent.womplex.ibm.com/ibm.html

You can search by keywords, patent numbers, inventor, assignee, class numbers, etc. Images from patents issued since 1980 can be viewed online.

Search suggestion:

1 search by keyword;
2 find a promising title;
3 click on the (hypertext) patent number for the full entry;
4 click on the international or US class numbers to find other patents in the same area.

In addition, the US Patent and Trademark Office offers a freely searchable database of front page information (but with no images) from patents issued since 1976:

US Patent Bibliographic Database

http://patents.uspto.gov/patbib_index.html

Another free indexing service is available from the Internet Patent News Service. US patent titles since 1970 can be retrieved online using the *Manual of Classification*:

http://sunsite.unc.edu/patents/

6.5 STATISTICS AND MARKET DATA

At some stage during a project you might need statistical data to support an argument, investigate market potential, analyse past failures, forecast social or economic trends, and so on. Series of statistics and market data can tell you what happened in the past, what is happening now and what might happen in the future. The Office for National Statistics claims that its data 'can help you to monitor business trends, identify successful products, assess your efficiency, identify new markets'.

The detailed financial data and business ratios offered by some of the commercially produced market surveys provide both an overall profile of an industry and a means of comparing competing companies within it. However, some of the market surveys are expensive to buy and difficult to get hold of through libraries. This makes the service provided by the SRIS Business Information Service at Holborn particularly valuable (see their listing *Market Research* below). Many reports are also available on loan from the Document Supply Centre at Boston Spa.

The government (through the Office for National Statistics and individual Departments) is the most important source of social, economic, consumer and industrial statistics. Industry and product surveys carried out by commercial organizations, trade associations and academic bodies are, however, sometimes generally available. In the nature of things, printed statistics cannot be absolutely up-to-date, but they should be current enough to support a proposal in a report, indicate a trend, or whatever.

Out of the mass of published statistics, the larger public libraries will have many of the standard government series. For more specialized data and privately conducted market surveys, you would need to go to the large business libraries or appropriate special organizations (Sections 4 and 7), or use a computer database (Section 5.6).

Although the Internet has in the past tended to disappoint as a source of statistics, many more are now appearing – some sources are given below.

In addition to the sources given in this section, many reference books contain statistical information. For example, the *Euromonitor Regional Handbooks* contain a great deal of statistical data.

Many statistical series, particularly if produced abroad, may present problems of interpretation. Differing product definitions, units, and so on, can, for example, cause difficulties of 'fit'.

United Kingdom

General series

Each government department publishes its own statistics (see the sources given below in 'Tracing statistics' for more information) but many of these appear later, perhaps in summarized form, in the general statistical series.

It is to these easily found general series that you would probably turn first for demographic, social and economic data:

Annual Abstract of Statistics;

Digest of Welsh Statistics, annual;

Economic Trends, monthly;

Monthly Digest of Statistics;

Northern Ireland Digest of Statistics;

Population Trends;

CD*Regional Trends,* annual;

Scottish Abstract of Statistics, annual;

CD*Social Trends,* annual (wide range of social and demographic data);

United Kingdom National Accounts, annual (the *'Blue Book';* 'Personal sector' tables cover household income and expenditure and consumers' expenditure by commodity and function);

Welsh Economic Trends;

Welsh Social Trends, every two years.

Specialized series

More specialized series cover subjects like energy, environment and transport.

Digest of Environmental Protection and Water Statistics;

Digest of UK Energy Statistics;

Energy Trends;

National Food Survey;

National Travel Surveys;

Road Traffic Statistics Great Britain;

Transport Statistics Great Britain.

R and D in science and technology, previously covered in the Office of Science and Technology's *Forward Look,* is now dealt with in detail in:

Department of Trade and Industry, Office of Science and Technology (1997), *Science, Engineering and Technology, Statistics 1997,* Cm 3695, The Stationery Office.

This has 69 tables covering government expenditure, R and D in UK businesses, gross domestic expenditure on R and D, international expenditure, and personnel.

The figures are also available on the Internet – go to the government's web pages and click on 'Organizational Index':

http://www.open.gov.uk/

Explore these pages, too, to investigate what other statistics the government might be making available on the Internet.

The Office for National Statistics supplies some time series on its web site. At the time of writing, these correspond to those in its annual publication *United Kingdom in Figures* and are not very up-to-date:

http://www.ons.gov.uk/

Industrial production and markets

> *Family Expenditure Survey*, annual, Stationery Office (patterns of income and expenditure of different types of household; product breakdown to level of, e.g., 'Television, radio and musical instruments'; regional variations).
>
> ^{CD} *PACSTAT: Production and Construction Statistics: Data for 1993 and 1994*, The Stationery Office (data from the ONS sample inquiries for 1993 and 1994, with data for the main variables for 1986–1992; industries grouped according to the *Standard Industrial Classification 1992*; tables, charts and maps).
>
> ^{CD} *UK Markets,* The Stationery Office (comprises annual and quarterly reports on the UK manufacturing industry's sales, export/import and net supply; one annual disc (containing the annual reports) and four quarterly discs (each containing the reports of one of the four quarters).

There are also several series of commercially produced regional, industry or product surveys, for example:

> *,CD *ICC Key Note Reports* (regularly updated reports on over 150 industries and products; industry structure, market structure, size and trends, recent developments, future prospects, financial data, industry and inter-company comparisons);
>
> *Market Profiles,* annual, Headland Business Information (market size and prospects for UK consumer, industrial and service market sectors);
>
> Mintel (periodicals include *Leisure Intelligence, Retail Intelligence* and *Market Intelligence*) also issue various special reports; information on market sizes and trends, brand shares, new developments, competitive trends, and so on.

See below, 'Tracing statistics and market data', for more on locating these.

A handy source for a wide range of mostly UK marketing data is:

> *Marketing Pocket Book 1998* (1997) NTC Publications.

European and International

European and international data are conveniently summarized in:

> ^{CD} *Consumer Europe*, annual, Euromonitor (230 consumer goods markets in 17 countries; covers demographics, economics, consumer expenditure, retail sales; publications in the same series cover Japan, Asia, China, Eastern Europe, Southern Europe and Latin America; CD-Rom is *World Consumer Markets*);
>
> ^{CD} *Consumer International*, annual, Euromonitor (24 countries; consistently expressed data on many markets; market size, population trends, economic indicators, consumer expenditure America; CD-Rom is *World Consumer Markets*);
>
> ^{CD} *Economist Intelligence Unit Reports* (usually quite broad subjects, e.g. *European Motor Business, The New Russia, EIU European Yearbook*);
>
> *Euromonitor Market Reports, Databooks and Strategy 2000 Reports* (cover regional and global markets for over 100 products and services; include statistical and original survey data; five-year trends and forecasts);

> CD *European Marketing Data and Statistics*, annual, Euromonitor (covers 32 countries; demographic trends and forecasts, employment, production, trade, economy, living standards, consumption, market sizes, retailing, consumer expenditure, housing, health and education, culture and mass media, communications, travel and tourism; CD-Rom is *World Marketing Data and Statistics*);
>
> *International Marketing Data and Statistics,* annual, Euromonitor (all countries outside Europe; population and demographics, production of agricultural and manufactured goods, overseas trade, economic indicators, standard of living, consumption, market sizes, retailing, consumer expenditure, housing, health and education, communications, travel and tourism; CD-Rom *World Marketing Data and Statistics*).

Official European Union statistics are contained in:

> CD *Eurostat Yearbook,* Eurostat (10 year time series covering demography, employment, housing, land and the environment, economics, industry, energy, etc.)

and there is a handy source of general European statistics:

> *Basic Statistics of the Community: Comparison with the Principal Partners of the Community*, annual, Eurostat (also includes figures for the United States, Canada, Japan and Switzerland).

The Eurostat web site provides 'the main EU statistical indicators online':

> http://Europa.eu.int/eurostat.html

Also on the Internet, *Europages* offers 'a selection of tables, maps and graphs which represent the key figures and main trends for each of the 21 Europages sectors', which include Agriculture, Energy, Metallurgy, Vehicles, IT and telecommunications, Electronic equipment, etc.:

> http://www.europages.com/business-info-en.html

Many libraries, including of course the specialized statistical ones but also some public libraries, keep series prepared by the following organizations:

> Organization for Economic Co-operation and Development (*Economic Outlook* and *Economic Surveys* of individual countries, including the UK; recent trends and short-term prospects, economic policies, jobs);
>
> International Bank for Reconstruction and Development (*Social Indicators of Development, World Development Report, World Tables*);
>
> United Nations (*Demographic Yearbook,* global and regional *Statistical Yearbooks*, regional *Economic Surveys, UNESCO Statistical Yearbook*).

Most public libraries will also have series of **country profiles**. These contain useful general background information on the economies, business methods, regulations, and so on of the countries concerned, as well as the numerical market data being discussed here. Examples include:

> DTI Overseas Trade Services *Country Profiles*, DTI;
>
> Economist Intelligence Unit, *Country Profiles*, EIU; available on CD-Rom (Silver Platter);

Price Waterhouse *Information Guides*, Price Waterhouse (100 countries covered).

Pangaea ITC is an excellent Internet source of country profiles:

http://www.pangaeaitc.com/bizguide

International compilations in the highly convenient CD-Rom format include:

CD *OECD Statistical Compendium* (Data Service and Information) (220,000 time series, 1960 onwards, covering food and agriculture, development aid, economic indicators, employment, energy, science and technology);

CD *International Statistical Yearbook* (Data Service and Information) (600,000 time series from EU/Eurostat, OECD, IMF, UNIDO, Citicorp, etc.).

The US Census Bureau's International Data Base contains demographic and socio-economic data for all countries at:

http://www.census.gov/ipc/www/idbnew.html

To find international statistical data, a good starting-point is the Biz/ed 'gateway' (see Section 5.6.3):

http://bizEdnet.bris.ac.uk:8080/dataserv/datahome.htm

Biz/ed also provide a 'request form' to access the *Penn World Data* statistics covering 28 variables on all the major economies from 1960 onwards.

The OECD (Organization for Economic Co-operation and Development) provides access to various free statistics, via the following URL:

http://www.oecd.org/statlist.htm

The Office for National Statistics site provides a convenient list of links to statistical sources worldwide:

http://www.ons.gov.uk/

Addresses of some commercial providers of online market-relevant information are given in Section 5.6.

Forecasts

Forecasts are produced by governments (for example, the Bank of England, the Treasury); stockbrokers (for example Goldman Sachs (UK) or Morgan Grenfell (International)) and by other independent forecasters (for example, Barclays Bank (UK), Henley Centre, the National Institute for Economic and Social Research, DRI/McGraw-Hill). Forecast figures are collected and indexed in:

Worldcasts, quarterly, Predicasts (for each product or economic factor, actual figures are given together with a value for the projected annual growth rate).

Economic forecasts (Treasury, Consensus, Coopers & Lybrand's) can be found in Coopers and Lybrand's *UK Economic Update and Outlook*:

http://www.coopers.co.uk/managementconsulting/economics/economics.html

The Economist Intelligence Unit produces a series of *Country Forecasts,* available on CD-Rom (SilverPlatter). Most of the commercially produced market surveys contain extrapolated and forecast figures.

The Directorate-General II of the European Commission: Economic and Financial Affairs provides economic forecasts. Their home page is at:

> http://europa.eu.int/en/comm/dg02/dg2home.htm

Oxford Economic Forecasting provides the overview section of the current issue of 'World Economic Prospects Monthly Review,' and the 'Oxford Weekly UK Indicator' via its home page.

> http://www.oxecon.co.uk/

Tracing statistics and market data

If you want to trace a published source of **UK** statistics, then there is a useful guide:

> Office for National Statistics (1996) *Guide to Official Statistics,* 1996 edn, HMSO (subject groups; index; many hundreds of sources, including important non-official ones).

The *Guide* is also available on the Internet – go to the ONS site at:

> http://www.ons.gov.uk

There is also a useful, free, 100-page guide:

Government Statistics: A Brief Guide to Sources, annual, Office for National Statistics (from Press and Information Service, Office for National Statistics, Great George Street, London SWIP 3AQ; 0171–270 6363).

For official **European** statistics there are:

> *European Official Statistics: Sources of Information,* annual, Eurostat;
>
> *Eurostat Index: A Detailed Keyword Subject Index to the Statistical Series Published by the Statistical Office of the European Communities* (1992) 5th edn, Capital Planning Information.

For tracing non-official European statistics, there is:

> *The European Directory of Non-Official Statistical Sources* (1993) 2nd edn, Euromonitor.

Sources of market data, and official and non-official statistics on a worldwide basis are covered by:

> *Statistics Sources: A Subject Guide to Data on Industrial, Business, Social, Educational, Financial, and Other Topics for the United States and Internationally,* annual, Gale Research.

American series are covered by:

> CD *American Statistics Index,* Congressional Information Service (official publications);
>
> CD *Statistical Reference Index,* Congressional Information Service (non-federal publications, commercial sources, etc.).

For tracing non-official **international series** there is the:

> *The World Directory of Non-Official Statistical Sources* (1996), Euromonitor.

Series published by **international bodies** are indexed in:

^{CD} *Index to International Statistics*, Congressional Information Service.

These last three series are consolidated on a CD-Rom *Statistical Masterfile*.

For tracing **commercially produced surveys,** a useful list, particularly if you can visit the library itself to consult the original (often expensive) reports, is the Science Reference and Information Service's:

Market Research: A Guide to British Library Collections (1994) 8th edn, Science Reference and Information Service (subject listing of 3,000 reports on hundreds of industries in the UK and overseas; most reports available at the SRIS or from the Document Supply Centre).

Some other guides covering these surveys are:

*, ^{CD} *FINDEX: The Worldwide Directory of Market Research Reports, Studies and Surveys,* annual, Euromonitor (details of 8,400 published reports covering 12 broad product sectors);

* *Marketing Surveys Index,* monthly, cumulating subject index, Marketing Strategies for Industry (UK) Ltd. with the Chartered Institute of Marketing (comprehensive; useful detailed subject index);

Reports Index, bi-monthly, Langley Associates (wide coverage of business and market reports and surveys from consultants, trade associations, stockbrokers, government and organizations such as Mintel, Economist Intelligence Unit, and Euromonitor).

Sheila Webber's Business Information Sources on the Internet has a 'statistical, economic and export data' section. Biz/ed has a 'data' section which has links to services which provide statistics.

http://www.dis.strath.ac.uk/business/index.html
http://www.bized.ac.uk/

There is a special service which indexes sources of **forecasts** figures:

* *Worldcasts*, quarterly, Predicasts (for each specific product or economic factor, the actual forecast figures are given, together with the source of the figures and a value for the projected annual growth rate; online version is *PTS International Forecasts*).

Recent statistics might well have been discussed in the newspapers: see Section 5.4. The CD-Rom versions of newspaper files have made this sort of searching much easier than it was.

For official statistics, if you cannot find what you want in the library you are using, you could contact the following:

The Export Market Information Centre (Department of Trade and Industry), Kingsgate House, 66–74 Victoria Street, London SWIE 6SW (0171–215 5444/5), acts as a national reference library for the public use of overseas statistical series and market surveys;

The Business Information Centre, 64 Chichester Street, Belfast BT1 4JX (01232–233233) maintains collections of UK and overseas statistics and UK market surveys;

Office for National Statistics, 1 Drummond Gate, London SWIV 2QQ (0171–533 6262), National Statistics Information and Library Service open to the public;

National Statistics Information and Library Service, Government Buildings, Cardiff Road, Newport, Gwent NP9 1XG (01633–912973) for general and economic statistics.

If they cannot help you themselves, they will direct you to the appropriate government office.

There is a list of UK departmental 'contact points' in the two official guides.

For non-official sources, you could try:

Science Reference and Information Service, 25 Southampton Buildings, Chancery Lane, London WC2A IAW (Business Information Service: 0171–412 7454/7977) has a large stock of market surveys, indexed in their own guide *Market Research*; maintains an index of market data appearing in journals;

City Business Library, 1 Brewers' Hall Garden, EC2V 5BX (0171–638 8215) has a very large collection of business material, and is a public library intended to serve those who live, work or study in the City;

the other libraries mentioned in Section 4.

You might use the guides to libraries mentioned in Section 4. You could also contact appropriate trade associations (Section 5.5): they will certainly know of the important sources in their areas and very often compile statistics of their own.

6.6 TRADE LITERATURE AND PRODUCT DATA

Up-to-date information on new products will of course be found in manufacturers' catalogues, data books and leaflets. Apart from the value of such material for the technologist, they can also be useful for:

showing how others are dealing with particular problems;

assessing competitors' innovations;

generally keeping up with design and technological trends.

Naturally, attention will not be drawn in these publications to actual or potential weaknesses. For evaluation, go to the trade journals, or, at one remove, to the printed indexes such as CATNI (see Section 5.2) or to online sources (Section 5.6).

There is a collection of 30,000 manufacturers' catalogues and other product literature at the Science Reference and Information Service (25 Southampton Buildings, London WC2A 1BR; 0171–323 7477). For information on this and on regional resources, there is a (now rather old) guide:

Trade Literature in British Libraries (1985) British Library Business Information Service.

Technical Indexes Ltd. (Willoughby Road, Bracknell, Berkshire RG12 8DW (01344 426311)) provide a commercial service offering microform versions of catalogues and data sheets from 25,000 companies active in the UK.

Trade and research associations, professional bodies and, of course, companies themselves, will often have collections of trade literature and may supply data sheets, design guides, performance figures, and so on (sometimes working with customers on the development of a product). Suppliers often produce catalogues of similar products from different firms.

To identify suppliers or companies involved with particular products or services, use directories, especially trade directories (see Section 5.5 for sources of company information). Large collections of directories are held by:

the Science Reference and Information Service;

the City Business Library;

large public libraries elsewhere (Section 4).

Alternatively, you might contact appropriate professional or academic groups (Section 7) or attend trade fairs or exhibitions.

Trade journals aim to keep readers informed of the latest products and carry manufacturers' advertisements. Nearly all provide a service through which further information, data sheets, leaflets, and so on, can easily be obtained. Many regularly review recent trade literature. There are guides:

Barrett, D. (1996) *Business Journals at SRIS,* British Library.

World Directory of Trade and Business Journals (1996) Euromonitor.

Finally, an increasing amount of trade literature is becoming available on the Internet (see Section 5.6.3), where, as well as the usual technical specifications and product data, demonstrations might be on offer.

It is probably better to go first to appropriate 'gateways' rather than trying to find individual sites via search engines (see Section 5.6.3). For example, at the Edinburgh Engineering Virtual Library (EEVL) home page select 'commercial servers' and then browse through the subject classification to find relevant companies:

http://www.eevl.ac.uk/

Engineering Information Village (Ei Village) offers a 'technical catalog shop':

http://www.ei-village.org.uk/village/

click on the 'Industry Mart' icon, then select 'Technical Catalog Shop'.

The DIAL directories of UK engineering products and services are searchable at:

http://www.dialindustry.co.uk

The Business Information Zone, for those 'seeking UK-relevant business information, products and services on the Internet', also has a database of contact information for companies not on the Internet:

http://www.thebiz.co.uk

More sources of company information are given in Section 5.5.

6.7 REPORTS

Reports not published in the usual way (the so-called 'grey' literature) may be available from the originating body, from larger libraries or from the British Library Document Supply Centre (see Section 4). The Science Reference and Information Service's Business Information Service has a very good collection of reports (but allow time for reading, since there are sometimes restrictions on photocopying them). Up-to-date information may be found in this form, contained in research reports, survey data, and so on, and so it may be useful to know how to trace them.

Many abstracts and indexes (Section 5.2) and online databases (Section 5.6) include reports, and there are some dealing only with reports (and other forms of 'grey' literature):

> *, CD *British Reports, Translations and Theses*, monthly, British Library Document Supply Centre (wide coverage of the social sciences, business and management, and science and technology; all items are included in the *SIGLE* computer database (see Section 5.6.2) and are available from the Document Supply Centre).

The sources given in Section 6.5 for tracing market surveys (*Reports Index*, for example) can also be useful for tracing other reports. Subject bibliographies (Section 6.1) and the news sections of journals (Section 5.3) may refer to reports. Official government reports, of course, are often vital sources, especially in the policy field, although they can be quickly superseded. Official reports of this sort can be traced through the sources mentioned in Section 6.2. For less formally published reports, you might have to apply directly to the appropriate organization (Section 7). There may be a charge, of course, or problems of confidentiality.

For company annual reports, see the sources given in Section 5.5.

When applying for the loan of a report through the inter-library loan service, always quote in full any report number.

6.8 CONFERENCE PAPERS

Conferences are often a good place to hear of fresh thinking in a field, since people from different disciplines and occupations may be brought together to report academic progress or new approaches to a problem. The published proceedings can take a long time to appear, although publication on the Internet is beginning to help here (see Section 5.6).

Some abstracts and indexes list conferences separately, and index the papers like journal articles. There are also specialized services through which you can find out whether the proceedings of a particular conference have been published, whether there have been recent conferences on particular topics, or whether papers on your subject have been given. Most libraries will take one of these.

Some electronic sources are mentioned in Section 5.6. Two useful databases are available to OU students from OCLC FirstSearch (see Section 5.6):

> *PapersFirst*;
>
> *ProceedingsFirst*.

Conference proceedings can be searched for on the British Library's database, OPAC 97, via the following URL:

> http://opac97.bl.uk/

In cases where the proceedings have not been published, you can of course try approaching an author or sponsoring organization directly.

6.9 THESES

If you wish to trace a particular thesis or find out whether one has been written on a subject, then there are various indexes: for example, the already mentioned:

*,CD *British Reports, Translations and Theses,* monthly, British Library Document Supply Centre (wide coverage of the social sciences, business and management, and science and technology; all items are included in the *SIGLE* computer database (see Section 5.6.2) and are available from the Document Supply Centre);

and the even more specialized:

*,CD *Dissertations International,* monthly, University Microfilms International (Doctoral and Post-Doctoral: copies of the theses are available from UMI);

CD *Index to Theses with Abstracts Accepted for Higher Degrees by the Universities of Great Britain and Ireland and the Council for National Academic Awards,* quarterly, Aslib.

The *Index to Theses* is also available on the Internet (you need to register by returning the form *Use of Copyright Databases* to the Open University – see Section 5.6; you will then be sent an 'organization name' and password which you are asked for when you 'register as an individual user'):

http://www.theses.com/

Theses can usually be consulted in the sponsoring institution's library or borrowed on inter-library loan (see Section 4). 80% of UK doctoral theses can also be bought from the Document Supply Centre, Boston Spa, Wetherby, East Yorkshire LS23 7BQ (01937–843434) at a price of £42, paper, or £30, microfiche.

In some cases, the permission of the author or university may be needed before a thesis can be seen.

University Microfilms International (30 Mortimer Street, London WIN 7RA) issues free catalogues of theses on, for example:

Business and Management;

Management Science;

Marketing;

Operations Research.

7 Organizations

The first part of this section deals with different types of organization, how they might be useful to you, and how to trace them. The second part gives some names and addresses. N.B. The Internet can be a very useful source of information on many organizations – see 'Internet' in Section 5.6.3 above.

7.1 TRACING ORGANIZATIONS (DIRECTORIES)

Directories enable you to identify, locate and obtain information about particular organizations or to find a list of organizations or people in a particular industry, profession, place, etc. Directories for tracing company and industry information (company or trade directories) are discussed in Sections 5.5 and 6.6. Large collections of this sort of directory can be found in:

> the Science Reference and Information Service at Holborn and the City Business Library;

> the libraries of trade associations, government departments and professional institutes;

> the public libraries in large cities, in particular:

> | | |
> |---|---|
> | Belfast | Leeds |
> | Birmingham | Liverpool |
> | Bristol | Manchester |
> | Cardiff | Nottingham |
> | Edinburgh | Sheffield |
> | Glasgow | Holborn and Westminster (in London) |

> (but even the smaller public libraries will have some).

There are guides to directories, such as:

> *Current British Directories,* (1993) 12th edn, CBD Research;

> *Guide to Directories held at the Science Reference and Information Service* (1991) 3rd edn, SRIS (3,000 listed by subject).

> Shaw, G. and Tipper, A. (eds) (1997) *British Directories: a Bibliography and Guide*, Mansell.

There are similar guides to overseas directories.

Directories: general

Some widely found general directories are:

> *Aslib Directory of Information Sources in the United Kingdom* (1996) 9th edn, Aslib (comprehensive, useful guide);

> *Associations and Professional Bodies of the United Kingdom: An Alphabetical and Subject Classified Guide to Over 3,600*

Organizations (1994) 13th edn, Gale Research (also includes Chambers of Commerce, Trade, Industry and Shipping);

Directory of British Associations and Associations in Ireland (1996) 13th edn, CBD Research (useful and widely found);

Industrial Research in the United Kingdom: A Guide to Organizations and Programmes (1995) 16th edn, Cartermill International (covers government departments, companies, trade associations, research associations, learned and professional societies, universities, libraries, etc.).

There are many directories covering a particular subject or industry. To trace them, visit an appropriate library, look in the guides to directories given above, or use the general printed or online sources for tracing books.

Some of the guides to information sources (Section 6.1) list organizations:

The Macmillan Directory of UK Business Information Sources is good on trade associations and independent research organizations;

Croner's A–Z of Business Information Sources uses a loose-leaf format that keeps it usefully up-to-date.

Journals often publish issues with directory-type listings. Many of the trade associations and professional societies (see below) publish yearbooks, lists of members, and so on, or may answer queries on organizations in their field.

Many of the Internet gateways (Section 5.6.3) function as up-to-date, virtual directories of their fields, e.g. ENDS Environmental Links:

http://www.ends.co.uk/

Government departments

The government, in its role as a provider of published information, is dealt with in Section 6.2. You might also be able to gain access to the library of a department or official body in order to refer to material not available elsewhere, or you might contact one of the many units set up to assist industry. The Department of Trade and Industry's Internet site provides details of many such schemes (click on 'Business Support'), including Foresight, LINK, SMART, Energy Efficiency and Environmental Technology Best Practice, the Information Society Initiative, Biotechnology Means Business, special sector assistance, the Business Link network of advice centres, and so on:

http://www.dti.gov.uk/

Government Offices for the Regions bring together the former regional sections of the Departments of Environment, Transport, and Trade and Industry, and can be very useful sources of information and advice (see Section 7.2 for addresses).

Further information can be found in the general directories (see above), and in particular in the following:

Civil Service Year Book, HMSO (detailed information on personnel and responsibilities of government departments);

Guide to Libraries and Information Units in Government Departments and other Organizations (1996), 32nd edn, British Library.

The DTI's presence on the Internet has already been mentioned: other government web pages can also be useful – check the extensive 'functional' (i.e. subject) and organizational indexes:

http://www.open.gov.uk/

Finally, links to *Institutions of the European Union* can be found at:

http://Europa.eu.int/inst-en.htm

Quangos

Quangos (quasi-autonomous non-governmental organizations) can be found in the following rapidly expanding publication:

Councils, Committees and Boards: A Handbook of Advisory, Consultative, Executive, Regulatory and Similar Bodies in British Public Life (1995) 9th edn, CBD Research.

Sources of information of value to business can be found in:

Business Information from Government, biennial, Headland Business Information.

Companies

For remarks on finding company information, see Section 5.5.

Professional societies

Professional associations or organizations devoted to a particular subject are of course obvious sources of expertise. They will probably have specialized libraries which will usually be open for reference purposes to non-members (who may be expected to have tried public sources first). Most of the professional associations offer reduced-rate student membership, which will at least entitle you to use their libraries. They may run an information service, although a fee may be charged. Some organizations have local branches through which you could contact an individual to help with informed comment or suggestions. However, their attitude towards non-members varies a great deal. Outsiders such as business people, researchers, and so on, will find many of them very helpful, though a few perhaps not at all.

Some addresses are given in Section 7.2. For tracing more, use the general directories listed above. If you need to trace individuals, many learned societies publish Yearbooks or Directories of Members.

Universities

Universities are increasingly making themselves more open to access by outsiders and looking for ways to co-operate with local industry. They offer a wide range of specialized technology and consultancy services. Your tutor or OU regional centre will be familiar with the situation locally.

Universities with strong management interests include:

Aston	Cranfield
Bath	Durham
Bradford	Leicester
City University	Liverpool

London

London Business School

Loughborough

Manchester Business School

Oxford Centre for Management Studies (Templeton College)

Salford

Sheffield

University of Manchester Institute of Science and Technology (UMIST)

University of Wales Institute of Science and Technology

Warwick.

For detailed information on research in universities and similar institutions, see:

^{CD} *CRIB: Current Research in Britain,* 6 volumes, annual, Longman in association with the British Library (detailed register of research being carried out in universities, polytechnics and colleges).

For general information and for tracing individuals in universities:

Commonwealth Universities Yearbook, 4 volumes, Association of Commonwealth Universities.

A neat way of getting through to university and research centre home pages on the Internet is via the *University of Wolverhampton UK Sensitive Maps*:

http://www.scit.wlv.ac.uk/ukinfo/uk.map.html

7.2 NAMES AND ADDRESSES

This is only a very small selection. For a fuller picture, see the sources mentioned in Section 7.1 'Tracing organizations'.

European Commission

Headquarters: Rue de la Loi/Wetstraat 200, B-1049 Brussels (tel.: (32 2) 299 11 11)

Austria: Europäische Kommission, Kärtner Ring 5-7, AT-1010 Wien (tel.: (43-1) 516 18)

Belgium: Commission Européenne/Europese Commissie, Rue Archimède 73 / Archimedesstraat 73, B-1040 Bruxelles / Brussel (tel.: (32-2) 295 38 44)

Denmark: Europa–Kommissionen, Østergade 61 (Højbrohus), Postbox 144, DK-1004 København K (tel.: (45-33) 14 41 40)

Finland: Euroopan komissio, Pohjoisesplanadi 31/Norra esplanaden 31, PL 234/PB 234, FIN-00131 Helsinki/Helsingfors (tel.: (358-9) 6226 544)

France - Paris: Commission Européenne, 288 boulevard Saint-Germain, F-75007 Paris (tel.: (33-1) 40 63 38 00)

France - Marseille: Commission Européenne, 2 rue Henri-Barbusse (CMCI), F-13241 Marseille Cedex 01 (tel.: (33-4) 91 91 46 00)

Germany - Bonn: Europäische Kommission, Vertretung in der Bundesrepublik, Zitelmannstraße 22, D-53113 Bonn (tel.: (49-228) 530 09-0)

Germany - Berlin: Europäische Kommission, Kurfürstendamm 102, D-10711 Berlin (tel.: (49-30) 896 09 30)

Germany - München: Europäische Kommission, Erhardtstraße 27, D-80331 München (tel.: (49-89) 202 10 11)

Greece: Evropaiki Epitropi, 2, Vassilissis Sofias, GR-10674 Athina (tel.: (30-1) 725 10 00)

Ireland: European Commission, 18 Dawson Street, Dublin 2 (tel.: (353-1) 662 51 13)

Italy - Rome: Commissione Europea, Via Poli, 29, I-00187 Roma (tel.: (39-6) 69 99 91)

Italy - Milan: Commissione Europea, Corso Magenta, 59, I-20123 Milano (tel.: (39-2) 48 01 25 05)

Luxembourg: Commission Européenne, Bâtiment Jean Monnet, Rue Alcide De Gasperi, L-2920 Luxembourg (tel.: (352) 43 01-1)

Portugal: Commissão Europeia, Centro Europeu Jean Monnet, Largo Jean Monnet 1-10ø, P-1200 Lisboa (tel.: (351-1) 350 98 00)

Spain - Madrid: Comisión Europe, Paseo de la Castellana, 46, E-28046 Madrid (tel.: (34-1) 431 57 11)

Spain - Barcelona: Comisión Europea, Av.Diagonal,407 bis, Planta 18, E-08008 Barcelona (tel.: (34-3) 415 81 77)

Sweden: Europeiska Kommissionen, Nybrogatan 11, Box 7323, S-10390 Stockholm (tel.: (46-8) 562 444 11)

Netherlands: Europese Commissie, Korte Vijverberg 5, 2513 AB Den Haag (Postal address: Postbus 30465, 2500 GL Den Haag; tel.: (31-70) 346 93 26)

United Kingdom - London: European Commission, Jean Monnet House, 8 Storey's Gate, London SW1 P3 AT (tel.: 0171-973 1992)

United Kingdom - Belfast: European Commission, 9/15 Bedford Street, Belfast BT2 7AG (01232) 240 708)

United Kingdom - Cardiff: European Commission, 4 Cathedral Road, Cardiff CF1 9SG (tel.: 01222-371-631)

United Kingdom - Edinburgh: European Commission, 9 Alva Street, Edinburgh EH2 4PH (tel.: 0131-225 2058)

UK Departments of State

Department for Education and Employment, Sanctuary Buildings, Great Smith Street, London SW1P 3BT (0171–925 5000; public enquiries: 0171–925 5555).

Department of Economic Development, Northern Ireland, Netherleigh, Massey Avenue, Belfast BT4 2JP (01232–529900) (responsible for employment, industrial relations, government's relations with industry, industrial development).

Department of the Environment, Transport and the Regions, 2 Marsham Street, London SWIP 3EB (information: 0171–276 3000; the Energy Efficiency Office also deals with general 'green' issues).

Department of Trade and Industry, 1 Victoria Street, London SWIH 0ET (General Enquiries: 0171–215 5200; Innovation Enquiry Line: 0171 215 1217; Business Link Signpost : 0345 567 765; help offered to commerce and industry, sometimes without charge; the Business Link system provides one-stop advice centres, with Innovation and Technology Counsellors; SMART (Small Firms Merit Award for R and D) and SPUR (Support for Products under Research) schemes).

Office of Science and Technology, Albany House, 84–86 Petty France, London SW1H 9ST (0171–271 2000) (reports to the Department of Trade and Industry; runs the Technology Foresight Programme to identify technology and market trends and thus improve innovation & development in the UK).

Industrial Development Board for Northern Ireland, IDB House, 64 Chichester Street, Belfast BT1 4JX (01232–233233; Business Information Centre, including online services, open to the public by appointment).

Scottish Office Education and Industry Department, Victoria Quay, Edinburgh EH6 6QQ (0131–556 8400; Industrial Policy and Technological Division is responsible for new technology, innovation and small firms policy).

Welsh Development Agency, Principality House, The Friary, Cardiff CF1 4AE (0345–775577; Technology Transfer Department, Centres of Expertise information network).

UK Government Offices for the Regions

Below are the addresses of the headquarters. Specialized units might be at different addresses in the same or other towns.

East Midlands: the Belgrave Centre, Stanley Place, Talbot Street, Nottingham NG1 5GG (0115–971 9971).

Eastern Region: Building A, Westbrook Centre, Milton Road, Cambridge CB4 1TG (01223–461939).

London: Riverwalk House, 157/161 Millbank, London SW1P 4RT (0171–217 3456).

Merseyside: Cunard Building, Water Street, Pier Head, Liverpool L3 1QB (0151–224 6300).

North East: Stangate House, 2 Groat Market, Newcastle-upon-Tyne NE1 1YN (0191–201 3300).

North West: Sunley Tower, Piccadilly Plaza, Manchester M1 4BE (0161–952 4000).

South East: Bridge House, 1 Walnut Tree Close, Guildford GU1 4GA (0345–125431).

South West: The Pithay, Bristol BS1 2PB (0117–900 1700).

West Midlands: 77 Paradise Circus, Queensway, Birmingham B1 2DT (0121–212 5050).

Yorkshire and Humberside: City House, New Station Street, Leeds LS1 4US (0113–280 0600).

Professional societies

Chartered Association of Certified Accountants, 29 Lincoln's Inn Fields, London WC2A 3EE (0171–242 6855).

Chartered Institute of Management Accountants, 63 Portland Place, London W1N 4AB (0171–637 2311).

Chartered Institute of Marketing, Moor Hall, Cookham, Berkshire SL6 9QH (01628–524922).

CIPFA (Chartered Institute of Public Finance & Accountancy), 3 Robert Street, London WC2N 6BH (0171–895 8823).

Design Council, 1 Oxendon Street, London SW1Y 4EE (0171–208 2121).

Industrial Society, 48 Bryanston Square, London W1H 7LN (0171–262 2401).

Institute of Administrative Management, 40 Chatsworth Parade, Petts Wood, Orpington, Kent BR5 IRW (01689–75555).

Institute of Business Ethics, 12 Palace Street, London SW1E 5JA (0171–931 0495).

Institute of Chartered Accountants in England & Wales, PO Box 433, Chartered Accountants' Hall, Moorgate Place, London EC2P 2BJ (0171–628 7060).

Institute of Chartered Accountants of Scotland, 27 Queen Street, Edinburgh EH2 1LA (0131–225 5673).

Institute of Directors, 116 Pall Mall, London SW1Y 5ED (0171–839 1233).

Institute of Management, Management House, Cottingham Road, Corby, Northamptonshire NNI7 1TT (01536–204222; open to the public for reference; membership (part-time students £35, full-time £25) brings photocopying service (£3.52 per photocopied article for members, £5.87 for non-members), borrowing rights and use of a free enquiry service; 100 *Reading Lists for Managers;* 150 'practical, action-oriented' management *Checklists*; CD-Rom database *Institute of Management International Databases Plus*).

Institute of Management Services, 1 Cecil Court, London Road, Enfield, Middlesex EN2 6DD (0181–363 745) (productivity, work study, O and M).

Institute of Manufacturing, 58 Clarendon Avenue, Royal Leamington Spa, Warwickshire CV32 4SA (01926–554498).

Institute of Personnel and Development, 35 Camp Road, London SW19 4UX (0181–946 9100).

Institute of Practitioners in Advertising, 44 Belgrave Square, London SW1X 8QS (0171–235 7020).

Institute of Public Relations, 15 Northburgh Street, London EC1V 0PR (0171–253 5151).

Institute of Quality Assurance, 10 Grosvenor Gardens, London SW1W 0DQ (0171–730 7154).

Market Research Society, 15 Northburgh Street, London EC1V 0AH (0171–490 4911).

Royal Institute of British Architects, 66 Portland Place, London W1N 4AD (Sir Banister Fletcher Library open to the public).

Royal Society for the encouragement of Arts, Manufactures and Commerce, 8 John Adam Street, London WC2N 6EZ (0171–930 5115; interest in design, the environment and industry).

Strategic Planning Society, 17 Portland Place, London W1N 3AF (0171–630 7737).

For more names and addresses, look at the directories.

8 Case study: finding information on knowledge management

The aim of this 'case study' search (for information on knowledge management with special reference to the public sector) is to show how you can quite easily, and reasonably quickly, find background information and the titles of books and journal articles in a given field. I used widely available and straightforward sources taken from 'the basics' section (5) of this Guide. I have not edited out failed lines of enquiry: it is not unusual to waste time in a search for information, and it is important to know when to stop.

The sample references are to give you an idea of the sort of thing you can expect to find in the different sources and of how a file of relevant material can be assembled and a comprehensive bibliography built up. I have included timings to indicate how much time you might need to set aside for searching various different sources and thus to help you pick and choose among them.

If you follow one or two of these searches through step by step on your own computer, you will find that some of the detail has changed since I did my search – certainly new references will have been added to the database – but the process will remain essentially the same.

BOOKS

I wanted some general accounts of knowledge management to start with and looked first in the index to the *Encyclopaedia Britannica* hoping to find an article that would give me an overview of knowledge management. There were entries for *Knowledge, sociology of / Knowledge, tree of / Knowledge base,* but nothing that looked like 'Knowledge management'. The subject must be too new for the 1995 edition.

Turning to specialized books on the reference shelves of the library I was using, I found only one candidate that looked new enough to be of use, the *International Encyclopedia of Business & Management* (1996) Routledge. In the main alphabetical sequence, the entry read 'Knowledge: see Organizational Information and Knowledge'. This article had interesting sections on 'Knowledge-intensive firms', 'Converting knowledge into capital' and 'Organizations as knowledge and information producers'. There were 18 references in the bibliography, two of which were of particular interest:

> Harvard Business School (1994) *VeriFone: the Transaction Automation Company,* Harvard Business School, case 195-088 (this teaching case describes the organizational structure of Verifone and the methods used by its senior executives);

> Starbuck, W.H. (1992) 'Learning by knowledge-intensive firms', *Journal of Management Studies,* 29 (6): 713–40 (Starbuck defines knowledge-intensive firms and surveys the practices that enable them to learn).

The Harvard Business School case study might be difficult to obtain, but the *Journal of Management Studies* was on the shelves of the library I was using, and, apart from its intrinsic interest, the article by Starbuck in its turn had a further 42 references.

Already my network of references was growing fast – and the Starbuck article might well make a good target paper for finding recent articles on the subject via a citation search (see Section 5.6.1, and below in this case study).

Furthermore, the next article in the encyclopedia, 'Organizational learning', was of interest and included another 22 references, including more reviews and/or classic articles, such as:

> Brown, J.S. and Duguid, P. (1991) 'Organizational learning and communities of practice: toward a unified view of working, learning and innovation', *Organization Science*, 2 (1): 40–57 (Fundamentally important article ...);
>
> Huber, G. (1991) 'Organizational learning: the contributing processes and the literatures', *Organization Science*, 2 (1): 88–117.

Again, these looked valuable in themselves, they would contain more references to previous work, and I could use them in a citation search to carry my network of references forward in time.

The library I was using took *Organization Science*, and so in three quarters of an hour I had filed three useful articles and had the beginnings of a useful bibliography.

I had also made a note of phrases and terminology that could be useful in an online search:

> Knowledge-intensive firms
> Organizational learning
> Organizational memory
> Learning organization.

[45 minutes]

Moral: Good synthesising articles in books, even if oldish, can provide a worthwhile starting-point for finding out about a subject and assembling a bibliography.

Advice: Set about trying to locate/obtain the useful-sounding books and articles immediately.

ABSTRACTS AND INDEXES

My next step was to look for some more recent journal articles. The library I was using took *Top Management Abstracts* (Anbar Electronic Intelligence), which indexes, abstracts and grades good quality articles from a wide range of journals.

However, the individual issues on the shelves had no indexes and I soon found myself in difficulties trying to identify the right section-heading for tracing material on knowledge management: 'Corporate culture', 'Organizational change', Organizational structure', 'Research & Development', 'Strategy', even in my case 'Public administration', all might contain something of interest.

I might have persevered if I had had more time (and browsing through these abstracts might well have brought to light all sorts of things of interest apart from articles on my subject of knowledge management), but since time was short and I had access to a networked computer, I decided to search databases online using my keywords directly.

[15 minutes]

Moral: Be prepared to cut short unpromising or time-consuming lines of enquiry.

COMPUTER DATABASES

Choosing the databases

Looking at the 'core five' databases (Section 5.6.2), I decided *Wilson Business Abstracts* and *Social Sciences Citation Index* looked the most promising. Both have their short-comings, *Wilson* being business and management focused, but rather small, the citation index being large but covering the whole field of the social sciences. However, both contain important management titles and I could turn to the CD-Rom *ABI/Inform* later if I thought there was a glaring gap in my bibliography.

Searching *Wilson Business Abstracts* on OCLC FirstSearch

Having got through to the OCLC FirstSearch home page, clicked on 'Use FirstSearch' and entered my authorization code and password (see Section 5.6):

Selecting the database

I clicked on 'Business & Economics', and then on 'WilBusAbs' and 'Select Database'.

Entering the search

At the 'Easy Search' screen, I clicked on 'Advanced search' – I recommend this option if it is offered, especially for beginners, because almost always the display shows more of the available options and gives a clearer sense of how to enter a search. In the 'search for' box I typed in **knowledge management**. (See Figure 1.)

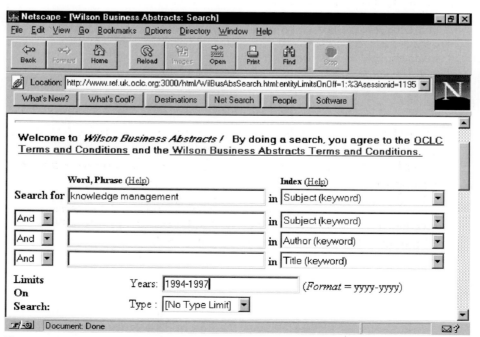

Figure 1

Setting dates

I scrolled down to the 'Limits' boxes. I already had some older material, so in the 'Years:' box I typed in **1994–1997**. (I decided to ignore the limit by 'Type' box because although I was primarily interested in finding journal articles, book reviews also might well be of interest.)

Entering a phrase on OCLC FirstSearch

I clicked on 'Start Search' and the system responded with the first 10 titles found and, at the top of the screen, the information 'Results=725'. This seemed to mean that 725 articles on knowledge management had been written in the last three years or so. This seemed rather a lot, and when I looked at the titles and saw some that looked totally irrelevant, I realized that I hadn't followed my own 'hints' (Table 5) and entered the phrase in the correct OCLC way, that is, with a 'w' between the two words: **knowledge w management** (without the intervening 'w', the system looks for records that have the word 'knowledge' somewhere and the word 'management' somewhere, but not necessarily together in the correct order).

Responding to initial search results

Now it was 'Results=40' and the list looked better. Here are the first few titles (as they appear after being saved on my hard disk as a text file – see below):

---

1. Getting to "real-time" knowledge management: from knowledge management to knowledge generation..
Source: Online (Weston, Conn.) Year: 1997 Tag Record
2. Facilitating knowledge management and knowledge sharing: new opportunities for information professionals..
Source: Online (Weston, Conn.) Year: 1997 Tag Record
3. Integrating intellectual capital and knowledge management..
Source: Long Range Planning Year: 1997 Tag Record
4. Assessing your company's knowledge management style..
Source: Long Range Planning Year: 1997 Tag Record
5. Knowledge management: a strategic agenda..
Source: Long Range Planning Year: 1997 Tag Record
6. Understanding knowledge management..
Source: Long Range Planning Year: 1997 Tag Record
7. Battle of the buzzwords. (intellectual capital, knowledge management, and the learning organizations).
Source: Training and Development (Alexandria, Va.) Year: 1997 Tag Record

---

These were fine, but I thought there were probably more to be found. If I looked at the full entry of a relevant record, I should be able to identify the subject headings that the database indexers used and by re-entering my search in these terms (the database's own terms, so to speak), I should be able to retrieve more relevant material.

Title 7 looked liked a promising source of subject headings: by clicking on the highlighted title, I brought up the full record:

> AUTHOR: Benson, George.
> TITLE: Battle of the buzzwords. (intellectual capital, knowledge management, and the learning organizations)
> SOURCE: Training and Development (Alexandria, Va.) v. 51 (July '97) p. 51-2
> STANDARD NO: 1055-9760
> RECORD TYPE: art
> CONTENTS: feature article
> ABSTRACT: National HRD Executive Surveys conducted over the past four years by the American Society for Training and Development provide evidence that the terms learning organization, intellectual capital, and knowledge management are more than buzzwords. The results of the surveys indicate that there is a significant overlap in the three concepts. The results also offer a perspective on how organizations are managing learning more actively than in the past and show that HRD professionals are championing and implementing those ideas. Details of the survey results are provided.
> SUBJECT: Learning organizations.
> Intellectual capital.
> Knowledge organizations.

All three of these subject headings looked relevant.

I went back to the Advanced Search page by clicking on 'Search' at the top of the screen, and in the 'Search for' box typed **knowledge w organizations or intellectual w capital or learning w organizations**. By clicking in the 'Index' box to the right, I could choose 'Subject Hdgs (Keyword)' – this will limit the search to those records deliberately indexed as dealing with one of those subjects. And of course I have also broadened my search by no longer relying on the author or abstracter having used the one phrase 'knowledge management'.

Introducing a second concept to the search

The system had now retrieved 303 records, which seemed rather a lot to look through. So I decided to bring in my second concept, the public sector.

Returning to the Advanced Search screen (by clicking on 'Search'), I typed in the second 'Search for' box relevant words that I thought would occur in the subject headings field, **public or nonprofit or government**, and again clicked in the 'Index' box and selected 'Subject Hdgs (Keyword)'.

But I'd overlooked another OCLC FirstSearch idiosyncrasy – a message appeared:

> 'You can only use two OR operators in one search. Try using History to combine results sets from previous searches.'

So, back at the search screen, I cleared the 'Search for' boxes, selected 'Subject Hdgs (Keyword)' and again typed in **public or nonprofit or government**:

This produced 10,259 'hits', but I hadn't yet combined the public sector set with the knowledge management set.

By returning to the search screen and clicking on 'History', I could click in the appropriate boxes, check that I was linking the sets with AND (i.e. that I was asking for 'any one of the 'knowledge' set with any one of the 'public' set'), and click on 'Search/Combine' (in Figure 2 , set 5 represents the intersection I asked for).

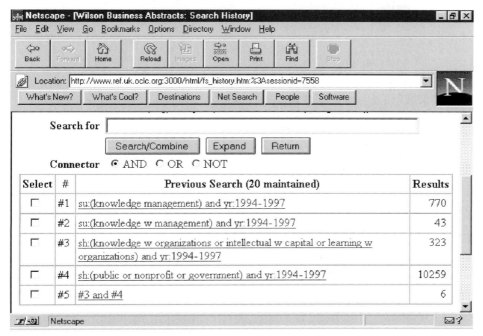

Figure 2

As often happens with this sort of search, from having too many references I had gone to having too few! Some of them looked interesting:

> 1. The measurement, use, and development of intellectual capital to increase public sector productivity..
> Source: Public Personnel Management Year: 1997 Tag Record
> 2. Education and training in the IRS today..
> Source: The Tax Adviser Year: 1997 Tag Record
> 3. Learning organizations and mentoring..
> Source: Public Productivity & Management Review Year: 1996 Tag Record
> 4. Institutionalizing learning organizations in the public sector..
> Source: Public Productivity & Management Review Year: 1996 Tag Record;

but I was not confident that the remaining 294 would not be of interest. For example, how many different keywords might there be that would be in some way relevant to 'public sector' – 'education', 'hospitals', 'charities', etc., etc.?

To avoid missing useful general articles, or even other 'public sector' articles, I would need to start looking through the 303. However, in most databases, titles appear in reverse chronological order, so that if I looked through one hundred, I would have seen the most recent hundred.

Assembling a bibliography

I went through the hundred, following the steps below (see Figure 3).

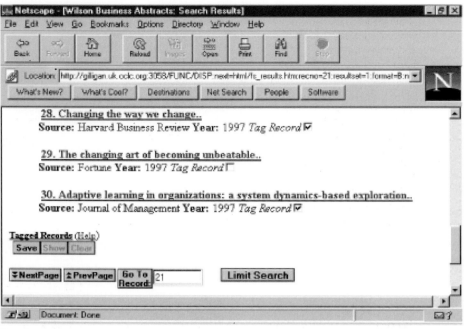

Figure 3

1. tag record by clicking in the box next to the promising title (click on the hypertext title if you wish to see the abstract)
2. after scanning each group of 10 titles, click on the 'Save' button under 'Tagged Rcds'

and only then

3. click on 'Next Page;

when the maximum of 20 titles have been tagged and saved:

4. click on the 'Show' button under 'Tagged Rcds', and
5. finally click on 'E-Mail Rcds' and enter your e-mail address.

The results are e-mailed to you with their abstracts (if available):

```
AUTHOR: Agor, Weston H.
  TITLE: The measurement, use, and development of intellectual capital
    to increase public sector productivity.
  SOURCE: Public Personnel Management v. 26 (Summer '97) p. 175-86 tabs.
STANDARD NO: 0091-0260
RECORD TYPE: art
  CONTENTS: feature article
  ABSTRACT: The use and development of intellectual capital offers public
    nonprofit organizations both a short– and long-term resource
    that can be tapped for improved productivity. Intellectual
    capital is the intangible assets of skill, knowledge, and
    information, and a program that tries to facilitate the use
    and development of such capital should consist of procedures
    for individual or organizational self-monitoring and
    regulation, the creation of new decision-making strategies or
    tools that hold promise for improved productivity and
    "mindware" for human brain skill, styles, or patterns. One
    tool that has been effectively employed by a big sample of
    public and nonprofit sector organizations toward this end is a
    Brain Skill Management Program, which is made up of three
    primary components: diagnostic testing, custom placement, and
    training in brain-skill development. To use such a program to
    develop and guide an organization's decision making process
    involves being committed to creating an atmosphere in which
```

> innovation is encouraged, prepared to organize groups and meetings in a somewhat less conventional manner, and ready to eliminate old management practices when they do not serve any productive purpose.
> SUBJECT: Intellectual capital.
> Government officials and employees – Productivity.
> AUTHOR: Grant, Robert M.
> TITLE: The knowledge-based view of the firm: implications for management practice.
> SOURCE: Long Range Planning v. 30 (June '97) p. 450-4
> STANDARD NO: 0024-6301
> RECORD TYPE: art
> CONTENTS: feature article
> SUBJECT: Knowledge organizations.
> Theory of knowledge.
> Theory of the firm.

....

[45 minutes]

Searching *Social Sciences Citation index* on BIDS

I was reasonably happy with the bibliography and thought I probably had enough material.

But while I was online, I thought I would do a quick search on *Social Sciences Citation Index* via BIDS. A search on BIDS follows a similar pattern as a search on OCLC FirstSearch, with two main differences:

- instead of typing 'and', 'or', 'not', you have to use commas to mean 'or', the plus sign to mean 'and', and the minus sign for 'not', so that a search will be typed in the form **(knowledge management,learning organi?ation*)+(public,nonprofit)** (see Table 4, *Searching the ISI citation indexes, IBSS & Ei COMPENDEX via BIDS: some hints*);
- the system's terminology uses 'check' for 'tag', 'mark checked articles' instead of 'save tagged records', and so on, but this shouldn't present problems (again, it is essential to 'mark checked articles' before going on to the 'next page').

Otherwise, searching a database on the BIDS system again involves filling in an electronic form and clicking on the appropriate buttons.

Choosing the database

Having got through to the BIDS ISI Easy Search screen (see 'Logging on ...' at the beginning of Section 5), I clicked on 'Advanced Search Form' (again, I recommend this for beginners because more of the available options are displayed for you on the screen). Looking down the screen, I could see that the system had defaulted to the *Science Citation Index* and so I altered the database to the *Social Sciences Citation Index* by clicking in the box 'Using the ... database').

Setting dates

Again, the system's default date range of 1994–1997 suited me, but by clicking in the 'from' box I could have selected any date from 1981 onwards (the starting date for articles in the database). Note that on the same screen you are offered the possibility of limiting your search to English (or some other) language and of specifying 'document type'. I was happy to take any document type, since a book review, for example, could well be of interest to me.

Entering search terms

My topic involves two concepts:

1   knowledge management
2   public sector.

As before, I decided to see how many references there were on the database on any aspect of knowledge management. If numbers were not too high, I could look through them all for relevant material. Using some of the phrases I had already noted, I entered the search in BIDS format, so to ask for records which contained either 'knowledge management' or 'learning organisations' or 'intellectual capital', in the box 'Search for ... in the Title/keyword/abstract fields' I typed

knowledge management,learning organisations,intellectual capital

and clicked on 'Run the search'. (See Figure 4.)

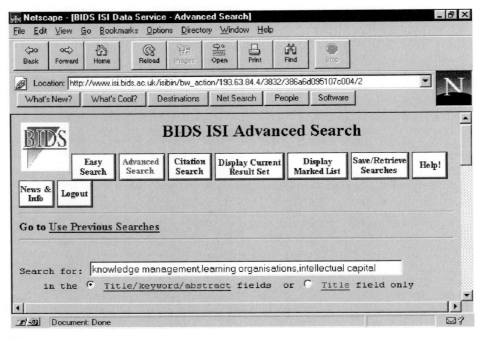

Figure 4

The system found 71 'hits', that is, 71 records where one of my phrases was mentioned.

Truncating search terms

But then I realized that I had not made allowance for singulars/plurals nor for the 's' 'z' spelling variant of the world organis/zation. By entering an asterisk, I could include all words with the stem 'organization', and by putting a '?' in place of the 's', I could allow for 'organisation' and 'organization'. So I clicked on the Netscape 'Back' button in order to return to the search menu and retyped my search

knowledge management,learning organi?ation*,intellectual capital

Responding to initial search results

Now my number of hits had doubled, to 177. This was rather a long list to scan, and so I decided to require the presence of a 'public sector' word. In effect, I was asking the system to go through the 177 records and retrieve only those which mentioned 'public sector'. I pressed the Netscape 'Back' button, grouped my 'knowledge' words together by using brackets and typed in some 'public' words. The search was now:

> (knowledge management,learning organi?ation*,intellectual capital)
> +(public,nonprofit)

Assembling a bibliography

This time the system came back with 11 hits. The pattern was the same as on OCLC FirstSearch: I had gone from having rather too many references to having definitely too few. Again, I couldn't ignore the 166 that would be left if I looked at just the 11. So I clicked on 'Use Previous Searches', saw that in the list of searches that I had done, the set I wanted was number 2, typed **2** in the 'use previous searches' box, and finally clicked on 'Run the previous search'. Now I could go through as many of the titles as I had time for (remember that they will be displayed with the most recent first), 'checking' interesting-sounding articles by clicking in the box to the left of each record.

N.B. References are offered in groups of 30 and if you have 'checked' any articles it is essential to click on 'Mark Checked Articles' not on 'Next Page'; the records you have ticked will then be saved for you and the next 30 references will be displayed.

Out of the first 100 titles, I ended up with 34 references of real interest. Here are the first few in the format in which they are initially displayed and as they appear saved on my computer as a text file (a full entry is shown below):

Copyright 1997, Institute for Scientific Information Inc.
(1) TI: Getting to "real-time" knowledge management: From knowledge management to knowledge generation
AU: Ghilardi_FJM
JN: ONLINE, 1997, Vol.21, No.5, p.99
(2) TI: Community youth development: Learning the new story
AU: Jarvis_SV, Shear_L, Hughes_DM
JN: CHILD WELFARE, 1997, Vol.76, No.5, pp.719-741
(3) TI: The importance of collaborative know-how: An empirical test of the learning organization
AU: Simonin_BL
JN: ACADEMY OF MANAGEMENT JOURNAL, 1997, Vol.40, No.5, pp.1150-1174
(4) TI: Cultural analysis, 'good conversation' and the creation of a multicultural learning organization
AU: McMillen_MC, Baker_AC, White_J
JN: MANAGEMENT LEARNING, 1997, Vol.28, No.2, pp.197-215
(5) TI: Understanding and valuing knowledge assets: Overview and method
AU: Wilkins_J, vanWegen_B, deHoog_R
JN: EXPERT SYSTEMS WITH APPLICATIONS, 1997, Vol.13, No.1, pp.55-72
(6) TI: Knowledge management: Where did it come from and where will it go?
AU: Wiig_KM
JN: EXPERT SYSTEMS WITH APPLICATIONS, 1997, Vol.13, No.1, pp.1-14

Output of results

Now the system had put my bibliography on one side for me. I could have used Netscape to print it out straight away (click on the BIDS button 'Display Marked List' to bring your bibliography to the screen; then click on 'File' at the top left of the Netscape screen and, from the drop-down menu, on 'Print').

However, I preferred to have the bibliography stored on my computer. Again, I could have used Netscape (click on 'File' and then on 'Save As'), but I would get a neater result if I asked BIDS to e-mail the results to me. So I clicked on the BIDS button 'E-Mail Marked List' and typed my e-mail address in the space provided. Incidentally, the format (that is, the amount of information given for each record) which BIDS offers at this point – 'Full record excluding citations and research fronts' – is the most convenient one, and will include an abstract where this is available:

Copyright 1997, Institute for Scientific Information Inc.
(13) TI: Organizational learning in non-governmental organizations: What have we learned?
AU: Edwards_M
NA: 5 MEDUSA RD,LONDON SE6 4JW,ENGLAND
JN: PUBLIC ADMINISTRATION AND DEVELOPMENT, 1997, Vol.17, No.2, pp.235-250
IS: 0271-2075
AB: Learning is considered to be an essential component of organizational effectiveness in all sectors-private, public and non-governmental. All NGOs aspire to be 'learning organizations', yet few have reflected systematically on the success in this regard. This article summarizes the experience to date of international NGOs that have prioritized learning as an objective, drawing out areas of both success and failure, and reflecting on whether there are any features that distinguish learning in NGOs from learning in other types of organization. A simple typology and set of tests of NGO-learning are presented, along with a series of challenges for the future. (C) 1997 by John Wiley & Sons, Ltd.
KP: INFORMATION

[25 minutes]

Conclusions

This search had taken 25 minutes. I had ended up with 34 potentially interesting references to recent papers and had them stored on my computer. (Incidentally, if I had done this search from home after 6.00 p.m., it would have cost me about 45p.)

I also noticed that there were surprisingly many articles that hadn't come up on my search of *Wilson Business Abstracts*. *Social Sciences Citation Index* covers many hundreds more journals and it was clear that I needed to look at both databases for a comprehensive literature search.

Of course, I still had to obtain photocopies of the original papers or find them in a nearby library, but I should be able to get hold of most of them without too much trouble either in the library I usually use, or at one of the big libraries in London (see Section 4), or by going to my nearest Public Library and asking them to apply for photocopies from the Document Supply Centre at Boston Spa.

Finally, I could always try a citation search on *Social Sciences Citation Index*, using as my 'target' paper the 1992 W. H. Starbuck reference I had found in the *International Encyclopedia of Business & Management* (see under 'books' above in this section).

N.B. If you would like to get an idea of how a citation search works, see the worked example in Section 5.6.1 – here too you could follow through the steps yourself.

Moral 1: take advantage of the databases available online: searching is usually quick and effective.

Moral 2: if you want to be comprehensive, or if you are not getting good results from one database, try another

ELECTRONIC JOURNALS

I would be able eventually to get most of the articles cited in the bibliography I was compiling, but decided to look at one of the collections of online journals to see if I could obtain an article or two immediately. As an OU person, I have access to the EBSCO MasterFILE Service and to the BIDS *JournalsOnline* Full Text Service (Section 5.3).

I tried to log on to the EBSCO MasterFILE – its 'Business and economics' and 'Public affairs' collections of journals had produced good results in the past – but ran into problems. The message came up:

> 'Browse is fully operational for both Abstract and Full Text data. Searches via some fields are not working correctly at present ...'

Browsing a particular title can be a worthwhile way of using these collections of full text journals, but in this case I wanted to search them all. I did not want to waste time doing a search which would probably turn out faulty and unreliable, so turned to the BIDS *JournalsOnline* Full Text Service.

N.B. To take advantage of this you need the software Adobe Acrobat – see 'Journals online' in Section 5.3, 'Journals – printed and online', for information on how to obtain this free of charge.

When I had logged on (see Section 5.3 – go to BIDS at http://www.bids.ac.uk, choose *JournalsOnline* Full Text Service; then click on 'registered users' and enter your Username and Password), the 'JournalsOnline Search' screen appeared.

I clicked on 'Help' (on the left) in order to check how a search should be entered:

- use the usual BIDS format, i.e. the comma and the plus sign for 'or' and 'and'
- use '*' to truncate (to select all words with a given stem) and '?' to indicate a wild card (i.e. to stand for any single letter).

The 'Back' button took me to the search screen again, and I typed **learning+organi?ation*** in the 'Title/Keywords/Abstract' box and clicked on 'search database'. The system responds with a list of all articles retrieved (Figure 5).

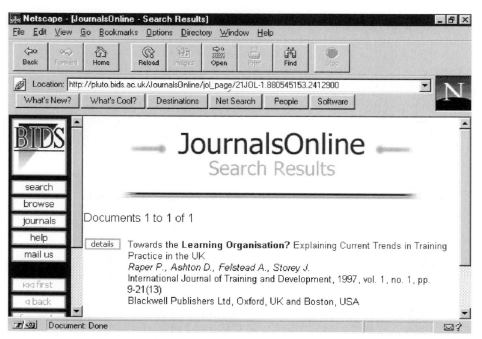

Figure 5

(I was not surprised that there was only article. This is not a research-sized database like the ones I had searched before, but a selection of the journals produced by only four publishers. As with EBSCO MasterFILE, what is offered is not the opportunity to do a thorough literature search, but the ability to retrieve and read immediately the full text of (*a few*) articles. Obviously this can be useful.)

I clicked on 'details', read the abstract and then clicked on 'document availability'. Unfortunately, 'Your library does not subscribe to this article...'

N.B. For OU students, the OU Library is 'your library': if the OU Library subscribes to an article on the system, an OU student can read it in full online.

I thought I would have another go, used the 'Back' button to return to the search screen, and this time typed in **knowledge+management**.

Again, there was only one article:

Documents 1 to 1 of 1
    Knowledge acquisition, modelling and inference through the World Wide Web
    GAINES B.R., SHAW M.L.G.
    International Journal of Human-Computer Studies, 1997, vol. 46, no. 6, pp. 729-759(31)
    Academic Press Limited, 24-28 Oval Road, London, NW1 7DX, U.K.

But this time, when I went through the sequence 'details' (for an abstract) and 'document availability', I was told that 'this document is available to you free of charge'. By clicking on 'Deliver document' and then on 'Click here to download the article', I could read (and print out) the whole article (Figure 6).

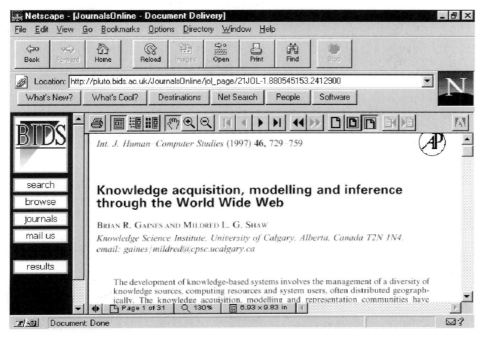

Figure 6

I had found a good article, but I might have found more in the larger collection on EBSCO MasterFILE if it hadn't been down.

Note: if you are following this search via an Internet link provided by a commercial ISP, you might find various hurdles erected. In particular, you might be asked for passwords before you can see the full text of an article from an Academic Press journal – these extra passwords have been passed to you with the BIDS ones.

[20 minutes]

Moral: if one or two articles on the spot are all you need (or you cannot get to a library), it is worth looking at the collections of electronic journals.

NEWSPAPERS

The library I was using had the *Financial Times* on CD-Rom and I was interested to see if the paper had recently published any articles on knowledge management.

The opening screen has three prominent boxes, 'Words', 'Dates', 'Info.'. I clicked on 'Words', entered in the search box **knowledge management or learning organisations**, selected 'headlines' from a list on the menu 'Specify where words should appear in the article', ignored the 'Dates' box, clicked on 'Done', and finally clicked on the 'Info.' box to activate the search (the details here do not matter – the point is that most of these CD-Rom databases are quick and easy to use).

There was one article for 1997 – the headline came on the screen and by clicking on 'text' I could see the whole (informative) article of 1061 words and download it onto my computer:

> ARTICLE 1 of 1 126 lines
> FT 97 Jul 14 / Management: The high price of know how: Effective knowledge management depends on harnessing expertise, reports Vanessa Houlder (1061)
> By VANESSA HOULDER
>
> Knowledge management is becoming one of the most fashionable management themes of the decade. Companies are attempting to create, share and store their employees' expertise in an effort to stimulate innovation and offset the damaging effects of downsizing and greater job mobility.
> Many organisations are acutely aware that they do not know what they know. Knowledge is dispersed in databases, filing cabinets and people's heads. Work – and mistakes – are repeated simply because there is no way to keep track of, and make use of, knowledge in other parts of the organisation.
> But although there is widespread recognition of the importance of knowledge management, discussions about it often get bogged down in philosophical abstractions. Hands-on experience of knowledge management is difficult to find....
> [the full text continues]
> ...Despite all the obstacles and costs associated with knowledge management, she argues that companies cannot afford to neglect the expertise within them. 'Managing knowledge is expensive but the cost of not managing knowledge is enormous,' she says.
>
> Countries:-
>   GB United Kingdom, EC.
> Industries:-
>   P6719 Holding Companies, NEC.
>   P8742 Management Consulting Services.
> Actuaries:–
>   Other Businesses & Services, Other Businesses.
> Subjects:–
>   Management.
> Types:–
>   MGMT Management & Marketing.
> The Financial Times
> Page 10
> London Edition 1

I had taken less than 10 minutes to scan through nearly a year of the *Financial Times* and go away with the full text of an excellent article. I could probably have done the same thing using printed indexes and microfiche, but it would have taken me very much longer.

[10 minutes]

Moral: it might well be worth finding out whether any CD-Rom versions of newspapers are available to you locally.

BOOKS

I knew that I could find a great many books on my subject if I looked at *WorldCat* on OCLC FirstSearch, but for the moment I just wanted to see if anything had been published quite recently which I might order directly online from the Internet Book Shop or look for in a bookshop.

The Internet Book Shop is at http://www.bookshop.co.uk. Clicking on 'Search' brought me to the 'Search page'. I typed **knowledge management** in the 'Title' box and clicked on 'Search Now'. Books retrieved are shown in broad categories (although you can choose to have them sorted by year or by price – cheapest first!). Seventy-four titles were found, including, under the heading 'Management and Business Administration':

> Management And Business Administration
>
> 5th Generation Management; Co-Creating Through Virtual Enterprising, Dynamic Teaming, and Knowledge ; Savage, Charles M. PaperBack £9.90 (Normal Price £12.37)
> A Guide to the Project Management Body of Knowledge ; Duncan, William R. Cloth £16.52 (Normal Price £20.65)
> Designing Team-based Organizations : New Forms for Knowledge Work ; Mohrman, Susan Albers etc. Cloth £25.95
> Information Management; Knowledge (TJ Bentley) ; Bentley, Trevor J. Paperback £12.00
> Innovation Strategy for the Knowledge Economy; The Ken Awakening (Business Briefcase) ; Amidon, Debra M. PaperBack £9.90 (Normal Price £12.37)
> Knowledge Based Manufacturing Management ; Kerr, Roger M. Cloth £36.00
> Knowledge in Action : Bata System of Management ; Bata, T. (Ed.) Cloth £37.00
> Knowledge Management and Organisational Design ; Myers, Paul S. Paperback £19.99
> Knowledge Management Tools ; Ruggles, Rudy PaperBack £11.00 (Normal Price £13.75)
> etc. etc.

Clicking on a title brings up the full ordering details – and I could order online if I liked.

The Internet Book Shop also offers to e-mail news of new titles of interest (scroll down any page where a full record is displayed for details).

In five minutes, I had traced and taken details of some new books in my field (I could turn to *WorldCat* for older books and foreign titles, and to check book references if I needed to).

[5 minutes]

Moral: it is easy to trace (and order) new books online.

INTERNET

Finally, I decided to spend half an hour (and no more – it is very easy to get carried away on the Internet) making a preliminary reconnaissance of the web.

NISS NetFirst

Since time was limited, I decided to start with NISS NetFirst, where I would be searching a structured system of standardized descriptions of evaluated web sites.

Having opened my browser, I went to NetFirst (http://www.netfirst.ac.uk), clicked on 'Search Netfirst' and entered my username and password.

Entering a search on NetFirst

At the opening page, I consulted 'Help' to see how a search should be entered and found yet another variation – the system would read **knowledge management** neither as a phrase (BIDS) nor as 'knowledge AND management' (OCLC FirstSearch), but as 'knowledge OR management', which would be no use at all.

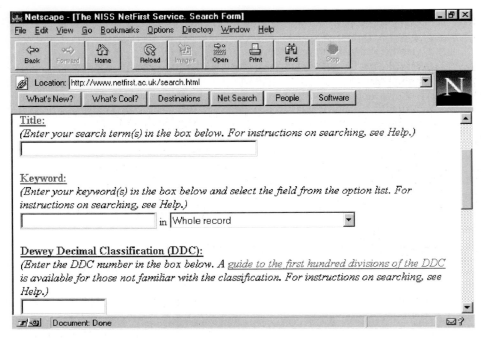

Figure 7

So I returned to the opening search page (Figure 7).

and:

> typed **knowledge and management** in the 'Keyword' box,
>
> clicked in the 'in' box to ask the system to search in the 'whole record' rather than just the 'summary',
>
> scrolled down to the 'Dewey Decimal Classification' box and typed in **65*** to limit the search to those records which had been classified in the Dewey area for 'management' (650–659), and
>
> clicked on 'Search'.

Search results on NetFirst

Here is the list of results, that is the list of web sites whose records coincided with my search profile (I saved it as a text file – on the screen all the site titles were highlighted):

```
The NISS NetFirst Service
Search Results
_____

Search terms: ddcnumber=65* and (knowledge and management)
Number of unique records: 22
Management & auxiliary services (65x)
   A Business Researcher's Interests (650, 658.0025)
   Business Research in Information and Technology (BRINT) (004, 650, 658.4038)
   Darden Graduate School of Business Administration, University of
   Virginia, (650.0709755481)
   Department Of Management Information Systems, University Of British
   Columbia (378.711, 658)
   Ernst & Young Center for Business Innovation (650.072, 658, 658.46)
   FID Knowledge Forum (658.403806)
   Fortuity Consulting (338.4765913, 658.83)
   ISWorld Net: Text Version (004, 005.75, 371, 658)
   Information Dimensions, Inc. Corporate Overview (658.46, 686.22544)
   Institute of Chartered Accountants of New Zealand: Library and
   Information Service (005.74, 657.092)
```

> Intraspect Software (338.470053, 338.7, 658.4038028553)
> Johnson Graduate School of Management at Cornell University (378.040974771, 650.071174771)
> Knowledge Management (658.4038)
> Knowledge Management (658.4038)
> Knowledge Management and Organizational Learning (658.4038)
> Knowledge Management: A Library Perspective (025.174, 027.69, 658.4038)
> Management Lab, Cambridge Technology Partners (004.068, 658.4038)
> Project 2000 Home Page (384.072, 658.84)
> Soundview Executive Book Summaries Home Page (338.7, 650.025)
> University of Phoenix: Bachelor of Science in Business Management (BSB/M) Program (378.1, 650.7, 658.4)
> What is Medical Informatics? (651.504261)
> grapeVINE Technologies Ltd. (005.3, 338.7, 658.4038028553, 658.46)
>
> © Copyright, NISS or original authors
> netfirst@niss.ac.uk, 25 November 1997.

This was quite a promising list. By clicking on 'Business Research in Information and Technology', I could see the standardized NetFirst description (again, I have saved this entry as a text file – on screen, the site title was highlighted to indicate a link):

> The NISS NetFirst Service
> Resource Details
>
> TITLE:
>   Business Research in Information and Technology (BRINT)
> SUMMARY:
>   Presents Business Research in Information and Technology (BRINT): A Business Researcher's Interests, an online information resource for business and management issues related to information processes, information systems, and information technology. Includes news releases and a FAQ section. Provides access to articles, papers, magazines, journals, and case studies on such topics as **knowledge management**, Intranets, electronic commerce, and organizational learning. Contains an events calendar and a site search form. Includes information on getting articles and papers published on the site.
> CONTACT:
>   feedback@brint.com host@brint.com
> AUTHOR:
>   Malhotra, Yogesh
> PUBLISHER:
>   Yogesh Malhotra
> LOCATION:
>   http://www.brint.com
> TYPE:
>   World Wide Web Resource
> TOP LEVEL DOMAIN:
>   com
> LANGUAGE:
>   english
> LC SUBJECT:
>   Information technology
>   Business
>   Information resources management
> DEWEY CLASS:
>   004, 650, 658.4038
> DATABASE NUMBER:
>   143505
> © Copyright, NISS or original authors
> netfirst@niss.ac.uk, 14th June 1996

Business Research in Information and Technology

This looked interesting. Clicking on the title took me to the site, where two of the alternatives offered were:

'Visit WWW Virtual Library on Knowledge Management';

'Participate in Online Discussion on Knowledge Management'.

The Virtual Library contained papers (many of them written by the author and publisher of the site), some bibliographies, and links to other sites.

I 'bookmarked' it. I could visit it again to take a closer look and to try to evaluate the quality of the material.

N.B. This process had taken about 30 minutes (although Internet searches tend to slow down throughout the day as American users come online). I had identified some promising-looking leads and would certainly return to the web.

[30 minutes]

Moral: if you're able to browse the Internet, do so – but it will pay to take a structured approach and to search precisely.

P.S. A note on the timings:
- they do not include time spent on obtaining articles on loan, travelling, and so on (let alone actually reading and digesting the articles themselves).

INDEX

Abbreviations, 18
ABI/INFORM, 51
Abstracts and indexes, **19–21**
   companies, 19
   market data, 79
   marketing, 19, 20
   newspapers, 30
   reports, 30, 79
   trade journals, 30
Abstracts in New Technologies and Engineering, 20, 54
Accountancy journals, 23
Acronyms, 18
Adobe Acrobat software, 28
Alta Vista, 62
AMADEUS, 34
Anbar abstracts, 19
Anbar Electronic Intelligence, 53
ANTE plus, 20
ANTE PLUS, 54
ARL Directory of Electronic Publications, 29
ArticleFirst, 52
Articles
   loans and photocopies, 14, 17–18
Asia
   companies, 32, 33
   statistics, 75
Aslib, 59
Association of British Chambers of Commerce, 36
Australia
   companies, 32, 33

BHI Plus, 19, 54
Bibliographies, 18
   guides to business information, 67–68
BIDS
   access, 37, 62
   citation indexes, 44–45
   databases, 50, 51, 54, 55
   logging on, 39
   search technique, 39–47, **99–103**
   training material, 46
BIDS JournalsOnline, 28–29, 51
   search technique, 103–5
BIRON, 57
Biz/ed, 34, 63
BizInfo, 35, 64
Bnet: Business on the Internet, 63
Books
   databases, 52
   loans and photocopies, 14, 17–18
   online catalogues, 58–59, 106–7
Boolean logic, 41–42, 47, 48, 49, 61
BOPCAS, 70
Borrowing books & articles, 14, 17–18
BOTIS, 14
BRINT, 35, 64

British Engineering Centre (Internet), 65
British Humanities Index, 19, 54
British Library. *See* Business Information Service, Document Supply Centre, Science Reference and Information Service
British Library Patents Information, 72
British Newspaper Index, 30
British Standards Institution, 71
Browsers, 60
BUBL Information Service, 63
Business and Industry (database), 28, 51
   access, 62
   logging on, 39
   search technique, 49
Business and management gateways, 63–66
Business Compass, 64
Business Information Centre, Belfast, 14, 79, 89
Business Information Service, 14, 31, 37, 38, 50, 73, 80, 81
   CD-Roms, 38, 51, 52, 53, 55, 56, 58
Business Information Sources on the Internet (Webber), 34, 63
Business Information Zone, 81
Business Link Signpost, 88
Business Monitors. See *UK Markets*
Business Periodicals Index, 19
Business Research in Information and Technology, 111
Business Webliography, 64

Canada
   companies, 32, 33
   statistics, 76
CAROL, 35
Catchword and Trade Name Index, 20, 54
CD-Roms, **50–59**
   Business Information Service, 38, 51, 52, 53, 55, 56, 58
   company information, 19, 20, 32, 33, 53, 56, 57
   conference papers, 55–56
   market data, 58, 75, 76
   newspapers, 30–31, 105–6
   product information, 20, 32, 57
   reports, 79, 82
   statistical data, 57, 58, 74, 75, 76, 77, 78, 79
   stockbroker reports, 56
   theses, 83
   universities
      research, 87
Chambers of Commerce, 36
Chartered Association of Certified Accountants, 89

Chartered Institute of Management Accountants, 89
Chartered Institute of Public Finance & Accountancy, 90
China
   statistics, 75
CIPFA, 90
Citation indexes, 20–21, 51, 55
   online searching, 44–45
Citing electronic sources, 9
Citing references, 8–9
City Business Library, 14, 80
Clover Newspaper Index, 30
Companies House, 33–34
Companies Online, 35
Company Guide, 32
Company information, **32–36**
   abstracts and indexes, 19, 20
   annual reports
      libraries, 14
   CD-Roms, 19, 20, 32, 33, 53, 56, 57
   databases, 53, 56, 57
   directories, 14, 32–33, 85
   financial data, 33–34
   Internet, 34–36
Computer databases, 37–66
Conference papers and proceedings, 82
   CD-Roms, 55–56
   databases, 55–56, 82
Consumer Europe, 75
Consumer International, 75
ContentsFirst, 52
Coopers and Lybrand
   forecasts, 77
COPAC, 14, 58
Corporate Financial Performance, 32
Country Forecasts, 78
Country profiles, 76–77, 78
Current contents, 21

D and B Europa, 32
Databases. *See* Computer databases and individual database names
Datastream, 38
Department for Education and Employment, 88
Department of Economic Development, Northern Ireland, 88
Department of the Environment, Transport and the Regions, 88
Department of Trade and Industry, 14, 69, 70, 85, 88
Design Council, 90
DIAL, 36, 81
Dialog, 38
Dictionaries, 17–18
Directories
   company and trade, 14, 32–33, 85
   government departments, 85
   on the Internet, 34, 35, 36, 63, 64

product information, 32, 81
professional societies, 84, 85
quangos, 86
research associations, 85
trade associations, 36
universities, 87
Directors, 33
Directory of Directors, 33
Disclosure United States, 34
Disclosure Worldscope, 34
Discussion lists, 65–66
Document delivery, 14, 17–18
Document Supply Centre, 14, 16, 81, 82, 83

EBSCO MasterFILE, **26–28**, 103
  access, 37, 62
Economic and Social Research Council
  databases, 57
Economics journals, 23
Economist Intelligence Unit, 75, 76, 78
EEVL, 35, 65, 81
Ei Compendex, 55
Ei Page One, 55
Ei Village, 65, 81
Ejournal Site Guide, 29
Electronic conferences. *See* Discussion lists
Electronic journals, 26–29
  search technique, 103–5
Electronic Share Exchange, 35
Electronic sources
  citing, 9
ENDS Environmental Links, 85
Energy Efficiency Office, 88
Energy statistics, 74, 77
Engineering UK, 36
Enterprise Zone, 64
Environment
  standards, 71
  statistics, 74
Europages, 35, 76
Europe
  abstracts and indexes, 20
  companies, 32, 33, 34, 35
  guides to business information, 67
  market data, 75–78
  professional associations, 36
  statistics, 73, 75–78
    databases, 57, 58
    databases, 57
  trade associations, 36
European Commission
  addresses, 87–88
  forecasts, 78
European Marketing Data and Statistics, 76
European Union
  Internet, 86
Eurostat (Internet), 76
Evaluating sources, 7–8, 60
Excite, 62
Export Market Information Centre, 14, 79
Extel Data, 34

F and S Indexes Plus Text, 53
FactSearch, 57
FAME, 34, 38, 53
Family Expenditure Survey, 75
Finance
  journals, 23
Financial data (companies), 33–34
Financial Times, 29, 34
  CD-Rom, 105–6
Financial Times (database), 106
Financial Times Information Ltd, 38
FINDEX, 79
FirstClass, 37
FirstSearch. *See* OCLC FirstSearch
Forecasting
  journals, 24
Forecasts
  growth, 77
  statistics, 75, 76, 77–78, 79
  Technology Foresight, 69, 89
Fortune 500, 34
FT Discovery, 38
FT Profile, 38
FTSE 100, 34

Government departments, 85–86, 88–89
  directories, 85
  Internet, 70
Government Offices for the Regions, 85
  addresses, 89
Government publications, 68–71
Government Statistics: A Brief Guide to Sources, 78
Grey literature, 81
Guides to business information, 67–68
  Europe, 67

Harvard Business School
  Baker Library, 36
    bibliographies, 68
    Internet, 64, 68
HotBot, 62
Human resources
  journals, 23–24

IBSS ONLINE, 54
ICC Key Note Reports, 75
Index to Business Reports, 30
Index to Theses, 83
Industrial Development Board for Northern Ireland, 89
Industrial Society, 90
Inference Find, 62
Infoseek, 62
Innovation
  journals, 24
Inside Conferences, 55, 56
Institute of Administrative Management, 90
Institute of Business Ethics, 90
Institute of Chartered Accountants in England & Wales, 90
Institute of Chartered Accountants of Scotland, 90

Institute of Directors, 90
Institute of Management, 14, 38, 68, 90
Institute of Management International Databases Plus, 53
Institute of Management Services, 90
Institute of Manufacturing, 90
Institute of Personnel and Development, 90
Institute of Practitioners in Advertising, 90
Institute of Public Relations, 90
Institute of Quality Assurance, 90
Inter-library loans, 14, 17–18. *See also* Document Supply Centre
International Bank for Reconstruction and Development, 76
International Bibliography of the Social Sciences, 54
International Business
  information guides, 67
International Business Resources on the WWW, 64
International market data, 75–78
International Marketing Data and Statistics, 76
International Standards Organization
  Internet, 72
International Statistical Yearbook, 57, 77
International statistics, 75–78, 79
  databases, 57, 58
Internet, 59–66
  bibliographies, 68
  business and management gateways, 63–66
  Chambers of Commerce, 36
  citing sources, 9
  company information, 34–36
  discussion lists, 65–66
  European Union, 86
  forecasts, 77–78
  government departments, 70
  government publications, 70
  International Standards Organization, 72
  journals, 26–29
  newspapers, 31
  online library catalogues, 13–14
  OU Library, 62
  patents, 72–73
  product data, 81
  search engines and gateways, 61–65
  search technique, 59–63, 107–11
  service provider, 37
  Stationery Office, 70
  statistics, 74, 76, 77–78
  theses, 83
  trade literature, 81
  U-Net, 37
  universities, 87
Internet Book Shop, 18, 58, 106–7
InvesText, 34, 56
ISO On-line, 72

JADE, 34
Japan
   companies, 32, 34
   statistics, 75, 76
Journals, 21–29
   electronic, 26–29

Kelly's, 32
Key British Enterprises, 32
Key Business Ratios, 32
King's Fund Library, 15
Knight-Ridder, 38
KOMPASS, 57
KOMPASS UK, 32

Latin America
   statistics, 75
Learning Materials Sales, 37
Libraries, **13–16**
   online catalogues, 13–14, 58–59
   statistics collections, 79–80
Libweb, 13
Liszt, 65
Lycos, 62

Macmillan Stock Exchange Yearbook, 32
Macmillan's Unquoted Companies, 32
MAID, 38
Mailbase, 65
Mailing lists. *See* Discussion lists
Major Companies of Europe, 32
Management and Marketing Abstracts, 19
Market data, **73–80**
   abstracts and indexes, 79
   bibliographies, 79
   CD-Roms, 58, 75, 76
   databases, 57–58
   guides to sources, 79–80
   libraries, 14
Market Profiles, 75
Market reports
   databases, 56
Market Research
   guides to sources, 67
Market Research Abstracts, 20
Market Research Society, 90
Market surveys. see Market data
Marketing
   abstracts and indexes, 19, 20
   journals, 24
Marketing Pocket Book, 75
McCarthy, 20, 31
Megaweb, 62
Metacrawler, 62
Microcomputer Abstracts, 55
Millennium UK Business Directory, 35
Mintel, 75

National Library of Scotland, 14
National Statistics Information and Library Service, 80
NetEc, 65
NetFirst, 62
   search technique, 107–10

Netscape, 59
Netskills, 60, 66
New Zealand
   companies, 32, 33
NewJour Electronic Journals and Newsletters, 29
Newsgroups. *See* Discussion lists
Newspapers, 29–31
   CD-Roms, 30–31, 105–6
   indexes, 30
   online, 30–31
NISS Business and Industry. See *Business and Industry* (database)
NISS databases, 50
NISS Information Gateway, 13, 62
NISS NetFirst. See *NetFirst*
Northern Ireland
   statistics, 74
NUKOP Online, 70

OCLC FirstSearch
   access, 37, 62
   assembling a bibliography, 43
   databases, 50, 52, 55, 56, 57, 82
   logging on, 39
   search technique, 39–44, 48, **94–99**
   training material, 46
OECD, 76, 77
OECD Statistical Compendium, 57, 77
Office for National Statistics, 73, 74, 77, 78, 79
Office of Science and Technology, 69, 74, 89
Official publications, 68–71
Online journals. *See* Electronic journals
OPAC 97, 14, 58, 82
Organization for Economic Co-operation and Development, 76, 77
Organizational studies
   journals, 24
Organizations, 84–91
OU Library
   web pages, 62
Oxford Economic Forecasting, 78

PACSTAT, 75
PapersFirst, 55, 82
Patents, 72–73
   Internet, 72–73
   libraries, 14, 72
   United States, 72–73
Penn World Data, 77
Phrases
   database searching, 43
Population statistics, 74, 75, 76
Predicasts F and S Index Europe, 20
Price Waterhouse
   Information Guides, 77
ProceedingsFirst, 56, 82
Product data, 80–81
Product information
   abstracts and indexes, 20
   CD-Roms, 20, 32, 53, 57
   databases, 57

   directories, 32
   journals, 25
Professional societies, 86
   addresses, 89–91
   directories, 84, 85
PROMPT, 20, 53
Public Affairs Information Service Bulletin, 20
Public sector management
   journals, 25

Quality management
   bibliographies, 67, 68
   standards, 71
Quangos
   directories, 86
Quest Economics, 58

Recent Advances in Manufacturing, 55
Reference citing, 8–9
Reports, 81–82. *See also* Company information, Government publications, Market data, etc.
   abstracts and indexes, 30, 79
   CD-Roms, 53, 79, 82
   databases, 52, 53, 55, 56, 82
Reports Index, 79
Research and Development
   statistics, 74
Research associations, 36
   directories, 85
Research Index, 20, 30
Resources for economists on the Internet, 65
Reuters, 38
Royal Institute of British Architects, 91
Royal Society for the encouragement of Arts, Manufactures and Commerce, 91

Science Citation Index, 21, 55
Science Reference and Information Service, 14, 72, 80
   CD-Roms, 38, 51, 52, 53, 55, 56, 58
Scotland
   statistics, 74
Scottish Office Education and Industry Department, 89
Search technique
   Internet, 59–63
Search engines and gateways, 61–65
Search technique, 6–7, **11–12**
   databases, **39–50**, 94–111
   electronic journals, 103–5
   Internet, 107–11
Share price information, 35
SIGLE, 52
Social Sciences Citation Index, 21, 44, 51
Social Sciences Index, 20
SOSIG, 65
Standards, 71–72
Stationery Office, 70
Statistical Masterfile, 58, 79
Statistics, **73–80**

CD-Roms, 57, 58, 74, 75, 76, 77, 78, 79
   databases, 57–58
   guides to sources, 78–80
   libraries, 14
Stockbroker reports, 34, 79
   CD-Roms, 56
   databases, 56
Strategic management
   journals, 24
Strategic Planning Society, 91
Switzerland
   statistics, 76

Technical Indexes Ltd., 72, 80
Technology
   journals, 26
Technology
   abstracts and indexes, 20
   databases, 54–55
   statistics, 57, 74
Technology Foresight, 69, 89
Technology management
   journals, 24
The BIZ, 35
The Times 1000, 32
Theses, 83
   CD-Roms, 83

   databases, 83
Tonic, 66
TONIC, 60
Trade associations, 36
   directories, 85
Trade directories, 14, 32–33
Trade journals, 26, 81
   abstracts and indexes, 30
   libraries, 14
Trade literature, 80–81
   libraries, 14
Trade names, 20, 32
Transport
   statistics, 74
Truncation, 43, 47, 48

UK Company Factfinder, 34, 56
UK Equities Direct, 35
UK Markets, 75
UnCover, 52
U-Net, 37
United Nations
   statistical series, 76
United States of America
   Census Bureau International Data Base, 77
   companies, 32, 33, 34, 35
   patents, 72–73

   statistics, 78, 79
      databases, 58
Universities, 86–87
   directories, 87
   online library catalogues, 13–14, 58–59
   research
      CD-Roms, 87
University Microfilms International, 83

Wales
   statistics, 74
Walt Howe's Internet Learning Center, 66
Welsh Development Agency, 89
Who Owns Whom, 33
Who's Who in the City, 33
Wild-cards, 43
Wilson Business Abstracts, 19, 51, 94–99
World Consumer Markets, 75
World Marketing Data and Statistics, 58, 76
World Wide Web. *See* Internet
Worldcasts, 77, 79
WorldCat, 18, 52

Yahoo, 35